October 2015.

# Flowers Bloom in Arid Soil

## JESUS IS THE GARDNER

Mona Knox Blandford

iUniverse, Inc.
Bloomington

**FLOWERS BLOOM IN ARID SOIL**
**JESUS IS THE GARDNER**



*iUniverse books may be ordered through booksellers or by contacting:*

*iUniverse*
*1663 Liberty Drive*
*Bloomington, IN 47403*
*www.iuniverse.com*
*1-800-Authors (1-800-288-4677)*



*ISBN: 978-1-4759-8605-1 (sc)*
*ISBN: 978-1-4759-8606-8 (e)*

*Library of Congress Control Number: 2013906846*

*Printed in the United States of America.*

*iUniverse rev. date: 4/18/2012*

I dedicate this book to my beloved hon Bob, who shared fifty four years with me

He walked with me all the way and kept me upright when I would have fallen. He was willing to move beyond his patterned ideas of God and Jesus to come with me into their presence. He too received the blessing and freeing of his mind and soul by being open to their calling to us.

I dedicate this book to Bill and Larry, my two sons who still call me Mom after all the mistakes I made in raising them. They are the main reason for this book. I pray you will find the joy and peace in the Lord that I have found. You are always loved with all my heart.

I am concerned about the world my grandchildren and great grandchildren will live in, and pray they can read my story and gain strength and find the Lord through these words. So I dedicate this book especially to those generations. Know that you are loved by me and the Lord loves you also.

I include those who have married into my family, especially Lisa my daughter in law of many years. My nieces and nephews, who grew up with me, are such an important part of who I am. All of you, thanks for walking with me on this pathway.

Of course I would be remiss to not thank my wonderful friends of all these many years, so faithful and true, so strong when I needed your strength. For all the tears and laughter we have shared, thank you.

# Table of Contents

# Introduction

A few years ago I attended a Lenten retreat. After a brief introduction by the mentor the first question asked was, if I were to die today what do I want my family and others to know about me.

That began another soul searching and set me once again on the path of writing my story. I have been thinking about doing this for some time. I knew it would mean going back into memories I would rather let lie, as they are painful. I also knew what God has done in my life should be told. My life has been so full, of good and bad, wonderful and horrible that I hardly know where to begin. A world of love, family activities, celebrations, grieving and all that happens to us in this world has kept me from being bored. At times boredom might have been welcome.

To make this easier to read, I refer to my husband Bob and my sons' father when I say Dad or dad. Boys always refers to my sons Bill and Larry and by name. Lisa is Larry's wife. All other proper names I might use are family members, grandchildren or other relatives.

And so I begin. Bear with me if I repeat some things, I think a certain point is important enough to be told again. Know that I do this out of love for all of you, my family, to assure you that God is real, Jesus is real and the Holy Spirit is real. My encounters with the Holy Trinity let me witness to this without any doubts.

As I have struggled for several years to put my story on paper for you to know what I have been through, the miracles I have seen and lived, visions, dreams and talking to the Holy Spirit of the Lord, it becomes harder each time I start to write. Some have told me since it is a witness to God's presence in the world I am being hampered by Satan. He would not like people to learn of the true stories which I have lived through and those of others. I don't know if that is so but I am constantly driven from the table where I write. I am going to use the computer to see if that will help me get this book written. People are praying for me and I have asked for God's guidance through this. I wouldn't want to make a false statement that would lead you to believe something that is not true. For those who don't know me, I don't make up stories and I do not have an imagination that could come up with the things that have happened.

It is a story that begins when I was a little girl and ends when I write the last word. I am now eighty one years old. I had another birthday since I started this. If I don't finish it now I might be looking at ninety years! For ten years I have felt pushed to tell about my life as a way for my family to become believers in the Holy Trinity, God, Jesus and the Holy Spirit. The truth is contained in this book and I promise you this, it will give you new ideas of what the whole world's story is about. Read it with open hearts and minds and find within these pages the truth and wonder of

God and His creation. May it bring you to a place within your heart that He has prepared for you for ever so long and where you will find a firm belief that this world is only a step in the right direction, of the promise of what is ahead for us. May God bless you and give you open minds and hearts as you read my story.

I have read ever so many books on religion, spirituality, faith and all manner of articles trying to explain the Holy Trinity. Too many are written as dissertations, for grades in college or to impress people with how knowledgeable the author is. Too often they are well written but rather vague about what they wish to tell us. Some are down to earth and tell us in plain, simple language that anyone can understand. I have chosen to write in the language I use every day, not to go to a thesaurus to find words that impress you with how smart I am. I want to tell you clearly how I have been impacted in my life by the presence of, the gifts from and the protection of a loving, forgiving God-Father, Jesus-Savior and the Holy Spirit- Comforter. It has taken a while for me to recognize that I am God's child. As such I am due all the gifts He chooses to give us. I want to help you understand that you are God's children and under His grace and love you have received everything I have received. You just need to know and accept what He has given you.

We need to be awake and watchful, seeing and hearing His presence in our lives every day. I can't tell you often enough how awesome the Holy Trinity is but if you doubt that, just look at the pictures taken from the Hubbell space telescope. I have heard of the music of the stars that talks about the rhythm of what we consider a void expanse, a system that moves in sync within itself, a living, growing entity that we can't begin to understand. That idea fascinates me. I choose to call the mind that has created this universe God! What form or being God has is not for my finite mind to grasp or I would be as smart as God. That is where Adam and Eve, even if you believe this to be a myth, got into trouble. It is a good example of how we humans think we are smarter than we really are and how we try to outthink God. He does have remarkable patience with us.

I just now stopped to read chapters 14 through16 in the gospel of John regarding the Holy Spirit. I looked at the book of Hubbell's telescope pictures again. In seeing these pictures of our universe and perhaps the edges of others I begin again to see how huge God is. The God of our past was a smaller, more definite God that we thought we could live with and even try to control, according to our understanding of what He wanted. In these pictures of space, which isn't empty, He becomes an awesome, indefinable God-one so far beyond my and your comprehension it is almost useless to try to grasp how vast His creation really is. How He caused it to be is not mankind's ability to know even though science tells us they have the answer. I refer you the story of dirt in another chapter. I ponder as to why He created us when I consider how we act towards Him, even to mocking His Son's brutal betrayal and sacrifice as if it wasn't necessary for our salvation. After all, we are able to do nicely on our own. You will read later what a huge fall it is from the top of the mountain of pride when we take that spill.

In the 1970's the comet Khoutek came by our planet, not close enough to cause fear but close enough to let us see how big it was. We had searched the night skies for a long time and couldn't see it, huge as it is. One night Larry, you and Dad drove out of town until there were no lights to interfere with seeing it. You found it and came back to show me where to look to see it. This was in January in Grand County, Colorado. At around thirty two degrees below zero I stood in knee deep snow to see this comet. It was so big it spanned the southwest quadrant of the sky, reaching from the middle of what we could see and ended over the Gore Canyon area. That includes the tail that comets have. When I finally saw it I was breathless for a time. I felt so small and insignificant, like a dot on the head of an ant in this universe that could contain such a large piece of rock. Since the Hubbell telescope has shown so much more I now can begin to grasp how much God means to us. He emptied Himself and sent His Son Jesus as a human to live as one of us. That He would do this is stunning enough but that He then died for us is absolutely beyond my finite mind's ability to understand. A love that would do this should not be shrugged off by us or thought to be unimportant. This has happened once and will never happen again. The next time Jesus comes He will claim His world.

So I write of times when I have known that God is real, Jesus is close and the Holy Spirit is here with us, as Jesus promised when He joined His Father. It still amazes me that His promise is true. Some say it only applied to the time of the apostles, others say we have been abandoned or some other tale to make us doubt the truth. Having heard the voice of evil and seen its face twice I know that there is one among us who would destroy our beliefs in the hope of destroying our souls. Do not doubt there is real evil, it is alive and well, causing great distress in a world that once was perfect. Don't dwell too long on that evil as to do so will give it power over you and doubt of the truth will set in.

# MATTHEW 11:28-30

"Come unto me ,all ye that labour and are heavy laden and I will give you rest. Take my yoke upon you, and learn of me; for I am meek and lowly in heart; and ye shall find rest unto your souls. For my yoke is easy, and my burden is light." King James Bible

# *Life as I Lived It*

## CHAPTER I

## *Setting Up My Box of Pain*

IN HER BOOK *GOLD in Your Memories,* Macrina Wiederkehr quotes Nancy Wood's poem, *The Beads of Life,* telling us the space between events is where most of life is lived. The events, good and bad, stand out in our memories more vividly than the day to day living out of our lives. We all have bad memories as well as wonderful ones, some too overwhelming to recall. I have very good memory recall and can remember too well some really ugly things that happened. I say total memory except for dates which I have trouble calling up for this story so it is not in chronological order. This thing about remembering dates has always been a problem so now I just write any date of importance on calendars and don't worry about that. Old age does have some benefits as we do as we please a lot of the time.

I can remember early childhood things that would be better forgotten. I have talked to people who suffered a lot of abuse in life and suffered a complete memory loss of events until later in life. Something would bring it back to give them great mental and emotional pain and harm. Some hardly survived this memory recall, coming back from what they call a split personality. In some ways I envy them their forgetfulness. Instead of forgetting I merely stuffed everything I couldn't deal with into what I called my box of pain. When something bad would occur I would mentally open it just enough to slip that incident in and quickly slam the lid down so no pain or anger could escape.

This I found in later years to be very unhealthy. It caused behavior that could have landed me in prison. As I look back I remember a gospel song which says, *pull back the curtain Lord, show me where you brought me from, where I might have been.* The truth of that hit me squarely in the face. When that happened I then had to deal with all the events that I had so carefully sequestered that made me a shy, fearful, miserable child. As an adult I was so eager to get along I would never argue with anyone but agree with one that the sky was blue and then agree with the next person that it was black. Without knowing what was causing this eagerness to please, I went along with people's statements just to avoid arguments or unpleasantness. I didn't feel my opinion mattered to anyone.

Going back into that box of pain was hard to do. As I looked at each event I had to relive it to grow past it. Some things took a long time to deal with but I came through that valley of despair and hatred. I found that by holding each event up to the Lord and sharing with Him it became easier to forgive and put it aside. By doing this I came to know that I was a victim of someone else's behavior. It brought me to a place where I could forgive each person who had harmed me. Some people say we should also forget but that is not in the Bible, just that we must forgive. In Matthew Peter asks the Lord how many times he should forgive someone up to seventy times. Jesus told Peter not seventy times but seventy times seven times.

I also found that I had learned a lot about people, their problems and pain. That made me better able in later years to help them find peace by praying with them to find the Lord in the heartaches they had suffered.

Healing of the emotions and spirit takes the courage to look inside and come to grips with knowing what happened. Things were bad. They hurt me in so many ways and I was angry and full of hate because of it. What a false face we present to the world when we deny our pain. We smile, act happy and try to be kind to those around us, ignoring what we really feel. Being civilized people we are required to act in certain ways that polite society requires for a person to be accepted. Most of us want to be liked by others.

The old idea that little children feel no damage from things done to them is so wrong. When a baby is born it is without knowledge of anything other than the instinctive ways to survive, eating and sleeping mostly. Being completely dependent on the adults who care for them, their minds are new. Minds that are a clean slate can be written on with dirty chalk that leaves ugly, scarring ideas that color their view of life.

I'm going to tell you what happened to me, when it happened and maybe why it happened to let you know that all the mean, ugly things that visit themselves upon us can be overcome. My relationship with God began at such an early age I can't remember, but I know that He was with me from the beginning of life and has been with me through one means or another until the day I say the last amen in my life. (Amen means so be it.)

I will try not to preach, I'm not a preacher. I'm hoping to teach although I am not trained as a teacher. I will try to teach through this witness, as it is called, that I am going to share with you. There are some really ugly times but also more wonderful times.

I will start with my being born smack dab during the Great Depression of the 1930's. I am the youngest of five children but only three of the older ones survived. A sister, Frankie Jean who would have been eight years older than me, died in a diphtheria epidemic when only an infant. All the family except my father had this disease that swept through Polk City, Iowa and probably in many other places. My sister Norma survived because our mother never slept and kept clearing Norma's throat so she didn't suffocate. The family was quarantined which meant they could not leave the house and other people could not come in. Food was brought in by my grandparents, who passed it in through a window in the pantry off the kitchen.

My mother couldn't bear the thought of her little baby being buried in the common grave that was being dug to handle all the deaths. She prepared the baby by bathing her, dressing her in her best clothes and then handed her out the pantry window to my grandparents. My grandma and grandpa Williams took her to a private cemetery in the middle of the night and buried her there. I have seen the place where her body lies but I won't tell because someone might decide she doesn't belong there and attempt to move her. Even though that happened in the year 1924 there may be people who would do such a thing. It really doesn't matter I guess. I believe that when we die our soul survives and goes to be with the Lord no matter our age.

Sometime after that my family of five moved to Colorado where I was born. My father worked in the coal mines in Routt County. Times were hard and what money was available he spent on gambling, alcohol and other things to satisfy his needs. He had been badly abused as a child and his father, my grandfather, had abandoned his family when my father was only four or five years old. I think it is because of this that he was so harsh and abused his own children so badly.

In the book of Exodus we are told that the sons of the fathers will be punished for generations. However, later in the book of Deuteronomy we are told that each person will only be judged (punished in those days) for what they have done, not what their parents have done before. I don't believe we pay for our parents' wrong doing, the sins are handed down from one generation to another by acting in the same way we are raised until someone breaks that chain and overcomes the tendency of abuse we live through as children. If the word sin bothers you I will discuss it in a later chapter and that may relieve your mind about what sin might be.

My siblings were eleven, thirteen and fifteen when I was born. I am sure I was spoiled by them and dearly loved too. We were poor but poor is relative when love is present and overcomes the lack of things. However all their love and care could not protect me from the abuse which I was to suffer.

As I write this first part I tell you only one member of my family ever knew from me what happened. When I was around age sixty five I told my sister Norma about two incidents. My father knew part of it but I am not sure if he told my mother. I don't recall ever being talked to about any of it.

Small children in those days were thought to just be playing until they grew up and gained some sense through schooling, or so it was in my family. They were to be seen and not heard. In other words when adults were around you sat still and kept quiet. This was true in most families.

As I write this part of the story for the first time ever it causes me to become very uncomfortable and sweaty even now. Although I, through the cleansing power of forgiveness have forgiven them with the Lords help, I still remember much too vividly those days and the days that followed.

I was between the age of three and four, probably the only small child and especially the only small girl in the immediate neighborhood. Other children lived close by and were seven to ten years old. Our little group of homes was on the edge of town and consisted of close to twenty houses. Some sheltered families and others were lived in by single men who worked in the mines.

One day I was invited to go with a group of boys who offered me a pretty something that appealed to me but I had to go with them to get it. The picture of that day is clear in my memory. The sun was shining, the sky was blue and I cheerfully went along with them into a vacant house. I had no idea what was ahead for me. When they told me what to do I just did it, not knowing anything was wrong. Little children are so trusting of those older than themselves, even though they too are children.

I don't know how or when my father found where we were and saw what was happening. Those boys were raping me taking turns. I am not sure if penetration took place as I don't know when young boys are old enough to do this. I don't remember pain at all so I question if actual rape took place. Perhaps they were acting like they were capable of doing this. I also don't know what my father did to those boys when he found us, as they scattered. I only know that my father whipped me on my bare legs with a willow switch which is almost like a leather whip. He hit me only when he could catch me, as after the first few blows I ran as fast as my legs could go to get home.

Neither father nor my mother ever said anything to me about what was wrong with this scenario, never explained what sex was. I only knew that I had done something really bad and was guilty of something. I didn't know what. We didn't get punished unless we had done something wrong.

Thus began years of feeling guilty about anything that happened to me or anyone else I knew. If a friend or family member was hurt in some way I felt it was my fault for not preventing it from happening. Kids' minds only go along with what they have been taught when young, even though that teaching might be very subtle.

I don't understand why people didn't watch their

children better but I guess they were so worried about making a living in this depressed area they didn't give much thought that kids would do such things. This happening to me may have made adults in my world more aware of what was possible.

Not too long after this occurred my mother and I were visiting a friend of hers. While they drank coffee and talked I went outside to play. The old bachelor who lived next door offered me candy and of course not having many sweets I took it, but only after he said I would have to come in his house for it. I can remember him carrying me and laying me on his bed and getting next to me. As young as I was I noticed how really dirty his house and the sheets were. Everything was an ugly gray color. Our house though cheap and poor was always clean.

He had only started to molest me when my mother called my name. I remember what went on as if it has just happened, from the time he laid me on the bed until he lifted me off and pushed me out the door. I am sure Mother saw where I had been and told me to stay away from him. I don't remember knowing I had been in danger. Apparently someone had a talk with this old guy as he never came near me again.

Today we tell our sons and daughters of the dangers that exist but in those days I wasn't told what the danger was or what could have happened. Once again I knew I had done something wrong and I was guilty. It was my fault because I wanted the candy.

This set me on a pathway of fear, guilt, shyness and being afraid to speak up on my own behalf. Somehow word must have gotten out about all of this because in later years I was teased about not being a nice girl. I was called ugly names by some and treated by some as being less than a nice person.

At this same time I was dealing with the death of a cat which I talk about in another chapter, witnessing the battles between my parents and their divorce. Add another layer of guilt because I had to have done something to cause this.

I was in contact with my father at times until he died. We didn't have a close relationship as he remarried and had another family to care for. My mother taught me that I didn't have to love him but must respect him as he was my father. She believed in the commandment that says to honor your mother and father. So I tried to be at least friendly with him. Had she not told me this I may not have maintained contact with him.

I soon came to realize there are really mean, nasty people in the world. They will hurt you physically, emotionally or mentally just to satisfy something within them or to see you cry. I learned at an early age to never let anyone see me cry as I knew it would tell them they could hurt me. Then they would just hurt me again. I also learned to hate!

With a deeply buried hatred that I would not let surface in action but nurtured closely within myself, I set up my mental box of pain and sorrow. As more sad things and events occurred I learned to stuff them into that mental box, slipping the lid off long enough to shove the newest pain into it and closing the lid again. In this way I shut out all the ugliness in my life. Not a very healthy way to live I can assure you. By doing this to my emotions I also almost killed any ability to fully enjoy happiness and good times. I would laugh and act happy but pictures of me show I am not fully into it.

I had a secret place to keep shut down. In my middle thirties that lid came off and all the pain, anger, even rage came pouring out into an action that I still find hard to believe I could consider doing. But for the grace of God I could have spent time in prison for killing someone. There were many more items in that box that had to be taken out, prayed over and finally released to get past the point of wanting someone dead.

I say this most firmly. No one has the right to take away the innocence of a child. I don't care that they claim they are unable to control their drives or whatever lame excuse they offer. The people who hurt children in these sick ways should be incapacitated so they can never harm a child again! I have heard others' stories that make mine not so bad. I don't know if counseling today helps heal these wounds to the soul of a child but counseling wasn't available then. Scars to the heart and soul never totally heal and will continue to impact one's life forever, or so it is with me.

As I grew older I managed to tell myself I was safe and to relax, no one knew what had happened to me. If they did know no one was mentioning it. Only in middle age was I able to deal with this and figure out that I was a victim and wasn't guilty of anything. This came about from finally finding Jesus in my life and knowing that if He loved me nothing or what anyone thought mattered. He accepted me just as I was, guilt, sin or whatever else I had carried all these years. That in itself was freeing but I still didn't want to have people know my dark history. After all these things are not for conversation over a cup of tea and cookies!

Kids are so cruel to each other and some never outgrow that cruel streak, perhaps because they too are carrying such deep pain and sorrows they can't deal with. The old saying sticks and stones may break my bones but names will never harm me has it backwards. Bones heal but names leave scars on the heart and mind. The cuts may heal but the scars can leave us wounded, timid and afraid. They cripple us emotionally and mentally so we can't recognize the gifts God has given us. We grow into very sad adults.

If you are carrying such thoughts and fears please know you too were a victim. You don't have to live with guilt you may have buried deep in your mind. You are as dear and precious to Jesus as anyone else and are just as good as any person on this earth in His eyes. Don't ever let anyone tell you differently.

When a woman in a Bible study said she didn't feel good enough to be forgiven the priest told her, if you aren't forgiven, no one in this room or anywhere else is forgiven.

To not accept His forgiveness is to say to Him, I am so bad you aren't strong enough to deal with it. That is telling Him you are bigger than He is! If we are to be judged for our life here on earth it will be done by Jesus. This is His domain. The final judgment is His exclusive job and as far as I know no one has been appointed as helpers in this job. He told His apostles to go out, teach and spread the word of the kingdom of God. He told the apostles to forgive those who confess their sins. I wonder if those uptight folks today who spend their time judging others will have to explain themselves to Him someday. Of course, when we judge others we don't have to look at our own faults, do we.

When I was around age four or five my mother divorced my father after all the older kids had left home and she only had me to provide for. She worked as housekeeper and caregiver for women who for health reasons were confined to their beds. I had to stay with my siblings for short times then.

Eventually we moved in with my aunt Myrtle and her son on their little ranch. Mom worked for our room and board by taking care of the house, the garden, the chickens and all the other many chores needing to be done. This helped my aunt whose health was failing. My cousin worked away from home which provided the money for us all to live on, along with what crops he would raise. One of the pleasant memories of that time was a ride in a sleigh pulled by a horse with bells on its harness. This was on a Christmas Eve trip of about four miles. We were all bundled up in blankets and warm clothes so it was a fun trip.

I started school while we lived there and had to walk almost a mile into town but other ranch kids would come along and we would all walk together. In winter we wore snow suits and boots, mittens and scarves that kids today wouldn't be seen in if they were freezing. We stayed warm. Times were really hard and our families were concerned about their kids being picked up by the hobos who travelled on the trains along side the road we walked. Men rode the rails as they looked all over the country for work as the Depression was still affecting most everyone. I don't know if the hobos would be interested in taking kids along with them but people were so worried, they might have just included this as something else to fret about. I was watched closely by the family when playing outside.

In October 1939 my mother remarried and my stepfather moved us back to Oak Creek, Colorado. I continued going to school where in first grade I became acquainted with a girl who today is still my lifelong best friend. Along the way another girl joined us and when we were freshman in high school another girl became a best friend. Only three of the four are still living and we still treasure this friendship.

However life in the good lane didn't last long. My stepfather, Papa Bill, was seriously injured in a mine accident when a chunk of coal fell on his leg and crushed his thigh. He spent many months in a Denver hospital. Mom and I lived on the coal miners' compensation which was a pension that barely kept us fed. When he finally came home he couldn't work as he could hardly walk and had to use crutches for a long time. We had to move back with my aunt and cousin for a time. Being young I didn't realize what a burden that was on everybody, although the house was so big we weren't at all crowded. As I have thought about writing this story I came to realize what an intelligent man my stepfather was and how he watched out for me all my growing up years.

My cousin had a hired man who to me was an old guy as his hair was white. He started stalking me and gradually became more aggressive until he was molesting me by groping and petting. I was seven years old now. My step dad must have caught on as to what was happening. He couldn't get around much so could sit and watch more than the others who were up and working. That action against me stopped. I don't remember if the guy was fired or we moved out. I don't know which came first but Papa Bill saved me from him.

One of the side effects of divorce in those days was that some people would not let their kids play with those who had divorced parents. I guess they thought we were tainted in some way. The women were preyed on by men, some single, some married. My mother-in-law, Grandma Dorothy who also was a divorcee, told me how she was hustled by one of the important men in town who was married and moved in social circles. She declined his invitation.

By now I was totally introverted, terrible lonely, unable to trust anyone except my family and my three best friends. I was afraid of everyone, especially males. Too guilty and ashamed to think anyone could possible like me, let alone love me, I managed to turn all my attention to learning all I could from books. They were then my good friends and I still enjoy reading books over any form of entertainment.

During the time at my aunt's I had gone to a Baptist church in Phippsburg and would walk to town on Sundays when weather was nice. I still have a small book of the Gospel of Luke from that church. A young woman from one of the families there had been a missionary and was visiting her family. She was going to walk to Oak Creek to give lessons on Scripture to families and share her experiences.

For some reason she invited me along. Maybe the Lord told her I needed to hear what she had to say. She had to come by our house and I was eager to do something different so I went along. This was a four mile walk one way but in those days it didn't seem like too far to go and didn't take us a long time.

I don't remember much of that day except the family we visited had children my age. Something she said, and I'm sure she was telling me things about God all the way there and back, sowed the seed that Jesus tells us about in the parable of the seed falling on good soil or bad soil. The seed planted that day by this young woman didn't sprout for a long time but didn't die either. I will tell this parable in full later.

As I write this book to share with you my journey with the Lord this is the beginning that I am aware of. What a simple thing for her to do and what an immense gift she gave me. God and Jesus were not spoken of often at that time but my aunt Myrtle, who was the closest I had to a grandmother, gave me a gold cross on a chain and a Bible with my name printed on the cover in gold. I couldn't read well yet I but liked looking at the pictures. I suppose both mom and my aunt prayed for me regularly. I didn't know about it or if they told me they were praying it didn't mean much as I would not have understood the importance of prayer.

And so my pathway of walking with the Lord is now in place. Many twists, falling off cliffs, and pure evil have caused that path to wander far from where it should have gone. If my story can help you deal with what life has handed you then it is worth going back through all these hard memories.

There are a lot of good times too. I can assure you God is with you as you have been covered by prayer since you were born. Don't let skeptics, false teachers and even theologians tell you differently. What is to come in this book will open your eyes to see the truth and be blessed by it. Remember, I don't have a good imagination so I can't make up these things I talk about. If I could do that I would write a novel.

In the gospel of Matthew Chapter 7, verse 7 we are told to not be afraid to knock on His door and ask for what we need, to stand at His doorway and seek Him, dare to ask to know Him. He is waiting for us to come to Him, He will welcome us eagerly.

I give you these verses to let you know it is not too late to seek, ask, knock on that door!

# CHAPTER 2

## *Reality Denied*

I WANT TO ASSURE you that along with the bad, hurtful things that happened, happy times, good memories and many good people were part of my life. The memories of those times and good folks warm my heart when I think of them. I am sure those kind, gentle people were instrumental in my finding my way to a better life and showing me a kinder side of life. Close family members who always let me know I was loved and important to them helped offset the misery. It is the best thing for us if we can concentrate on the good people who helped us along our journey in life. When we dwell too often on the not so good people and what they did, it gives them control of us even though years have passed.

Memories of living in small towns or on a ranch gave me the opportunity to wander through fields of flowers or go into the edge of the woods. The spring time smell of newly turned dirt, flowers beginning to bloom and trees getting new leaves is a gift too many of our young ones today never get to experience. Spring time in the mountains of Colorado has a special aroma about it and as the sun hits new growth everything seems to be almost magical. Columbine, Indian paint brush, shooting stars and so many other flowers make a picture city folks never see unless they make a special trip to the country. We kids could pick bouquets for our mothers, or harvest chokecherries for them to make jelly for the winter. I think that is still the best jelly to be found anywhere. (As an adult I have made many gallons of chokecherry jelly). I would pick service berries so my mom could make a pie. We were lucky to live so close to the forest. The berry bushes grew close to town and were covered with fruit.

Even so, those who had a nearly normal home life probably looked down at me for the ragged urchin I was. One fellow who was quite a bit older, told me at a town reunion that he was glad to see I had made it. I didn't care much for reunions after that as they reminded me there were people who knew my secrets.

All these spring and summer activities helped overshadow the bad. Winters were fierce, freezing cold with lots of snow. We all had sleds and the town's streets were almost all up one hill and down another which made for great sledding. Frozen ponds were available for ice skating. I would stay on the skating pond until I was so cold I would almost cry, struggle to get across town to home where my mom opened the oven door of the coal cook stove, and lay a towel on it. I would sit with my feet resting there until they got some feeling back. Of course my mother would also be on my case about not coming home sooner.

One lesson I learned when about twelve was to not confront someone when you are wearing ice skates unless you are a really good skater. A friend and her little sister were with me, trying to learn to skate. It was evening and we were alone on the pond until some older boys came by and started to torment us. They had a sled and kept trying to hit my friend's sister with it. I, being dumb but well intentioned, told one he needed his face slapped. He thought I wasn't big enough so I slapped him and he hit me on the jaw with his fist. I was flat down and saw stars as they ran away. End of that lesson!

I always took up for the smaller ones, the underdogs as they are called, ready to protect them but not as far as slapping them, unless I was big enough to get away with it. Today I still care a lot for the needy, the hurting ones. I even was a Brooklyn Dodger fan until they moved to California. They weren't the Brooklyn Dodgers anymore so I quit being a fan. I guess they weren't considered the underdogs anymore.

During my growing up years we received a good education. We went to class, sat down, shut up and paid attention to what the teacher was saying. I don't remember being taught about social niceties until we got to high school when dances, proms and such became part of those lessons. Social behavior was left to home schooling in those days and most parents taught their kids how they were to act in public. I remember being told if I got into trouble at school I would be punished when I got home. That was enough to make me behave at school, at least until high school when we all tested our wings to see how much we could get by with. The outcome depended on the teacher's mood as to how we fared.

We were denied lots of fun things due to World War II. Chewing gum was a wonderful thing then. Each store was given only so many packs of gum per week so if we were lucky enough to get a pack we would chew that gum for days until it was really gross. As I look back now I wonder how we did that. A song "Does the Chewing Gum Lose Its Flavor on the Bedpost Overnight" became popular then.

As everyone was in the same condition of life we didn't worry how we dressed or if we had the right kind of shoes and all the frivolous things we worry about today. We made our own entertainment with such street games as hide and seek, Red Rover, kick the can and others. Do those sound primitive. The games were good exercise and few kids had trouble being overweight. No one had money so I guess we enjoyed what we had.

I am always amazed that today's children are so organized and busy they don't have the time to just sit and watch the grass grow and day dream a bit. This does more harm than realized as it shapes them into ideas of having to always be busy doing something. There is a great big wonderful world out there for everyone to explore, look under rocks or watch a bee gather pollen, whatever is happening at that moment they are in. Can they sit and make mud pies, if there is a place not paved over so they can find the mud. There is so much to be learned just sitting in the weeds or tall grass and watching nature going about its business. To me this is how we should find the beauty of God's creation, not costing a dime but just being. You can't buy that joy as there isn't enough money to take it home in a box.

The memory of a pair of red rubber boots my aunt bought me is still dear to me today. As I waded in the small stream that ran by her house I would spend a lot of time just watching what stirred up from the bottom. I wonder what kids today will have for memories when they are my age and if those memories will be treasure or trash.

This reminds me of the songs we learned as teenagers, the ballads pretty much written to reflect the war time separations and the loss of loved ones. Those are the songs Dad and I danced to. I remember most as they stir memories of good times, falling in love and being romanced. The big band era has long passed. It is said that was the time of the best popular music ever. I guess each age group has its own type of music and thinks the same about it. We had silly songs too that seemed to lighten moods when war news became grim and disheartening.

Most entertainment was free as no one had any spare money. A movie once a week that cost us ten cents each was a real treat. We had picnics in the woods, slumber parties, not coed, which were fun. We cherished what we had. We knew how hard our folks worked to provide it for us.

We didn't hang out in groups much when in elementary school. Most had close neighbors our own age and two or four were best friends. As we got older we enjoyed being with groups and we would idle away time laughing and telling stories. A trip to the drug store for a soda was a special treat. After the war ended money was more available and we could afford a fountain coke.

I was a sophomore in high school before we got a telephone. I don't quite know what to make of the phone mania that persists today. I have a cell phone in the car for emergencies but I am never sure it is charged for use. The idea of being at everyone's beck and call at any time is not for me.

In high school we had a choice of business prep or college prep and boys had a Trades and Industry accredited class as a choice. We called it T and I. We girls weren't allowed to take that class as we were thought to be too delicate or some other weird idea. Today girls learn cabinetry and other ways of using tools. Girls also could not play organized sports like volley ball or baseball for the same reason. During the summer months we played unorganized softball and even had a team that competed with other teams. We didn't do well though as the other teams were all women who were better players. Today girls have most of the same teams as boys and do well in them. I was able to double track classes, taking business and college prep courses. This was almost the equivalent of a college degree today. It gave me opportunities to hold better jobs in later years which helped when we needed extra money.

Life moved along with some attendance at church for a time. I sang in the choir and when I was eighteen decided I needed to be baptized. I don't remember what prompted me to do this but I would suppose the Lord was still nudging me along on my pathway to Him. Dad and I went steady for a year during my senior year. Is going steady even a term used today. A month before we were to be married he gave me an engagement ring which I still wear. Seven months after I graduated from high school we were married in the Methodist church where I was a member and we set out on a lifetime journey together. We didn't have a lot to live on but we were both working and starting to do well. A year later we started increasing our family when you were born, Bill.

Some of the women in our town were so concerned if young couples had to get married they would mark the wedding date on their calendars then note when the first baby came along. Since our wedding day was December 30, 1950 and Bill was born on January 13, 1952 I would have fun telling people we were married in December and our baby was born in January, neglecting to add the years just to watch their eyebrows shoot up. After the desired effect I would then explain the years and try not to laugh too hard. I haven't said I was always nice to nosy people

Just a few months after we were married along came the first recession we managed to live through. A year later times were pretty bad financially and work was scarce for a long time. We moved around a lot looking for work and as a result we made friends in many places and I am still in touch with some of them.

Growing up in Oak Creek, Colorado, a coal mining town with several mines gave us the opportunity to get to know folks of every creed, race and color. There were extremes of elite or dirt poor of course but we came to know they were all just people and should be respected. When I worked at one of the drugstores as a teenager I waited on people who were considered the upper class of town but also waited on the ladies of the night and their masters. I don't think the word pimp was used then. All were treated with the same amount of respect as customers of the store.

## Chapter 3

# *Finding My Faith in God*

When Dad joined the Colorado State Patrol his first station was in Trinidad, Colorado. Today he would be called a State Trooper. We felt like we had been sent to the ends of the earth but found instead a warm welcoming community. By now we had another son, you Larry. I began to think about the necessity of finding a church where you boys could learn about the Lord. I didn't feel qualified to teach you. One evening while doing a Bible study that I had received through a mail-in card offer, I asked the Lord to show me what to do. Within a week people from four different churches were at our door inviting us to visit them.

Dad's supervisor and his wife invited us to an Inquirer's class at the Episcopal Church where they worshipped. My first reaction was we didn't have nice enough clothes to go to that church. I had always heard it was for the elite to attend. What a misconception that was. When Dad agreed to go to classes I was impressed enough to know this was where we should be. He was what was called unchurched and had always wanted nothing to do with churches. All he knew about religion was from hearing some of his family making fun of the hypocrites going to church on Sunday when they had been partying on Saturday. He had a slanted view of what church was about. I don't know why but he agreed with me that our sons needed to be introduced to church, so we attended six months of classes. We decided this was the church we wanted our boys raised in. Dad and you boys were baptized and then he and I were confirmed.

Some time in the past I had been talking to a friend about religion and we were saying we would never get on our knees for anyone like the Catholics did. God has such a sense of humor. He sent us to a church where we spent many years on our knees during worship in Episcopal churches. Fortunately for my old knees, today we have a choice of kneeling or standing or sitting if necessary

My faith was growing but still in its infancy. I was excited to find that God loved me just as I was and was always as close at hand as any prayer I prayed. I felt a new life had begun and all the old days could be forgotten. Our little family was doing just fine. I had made the commitment to God to try to be what He would have me be and to do the best I could for Him. This is the true definition of piety you know, to commit your life to living in God's way for us. People are afraid to make this commitment thinking it means a lifetime on your knees, keeping a pious look on your face at all times and never indulging in human behavior such as anger, love, fun or joy. Not so. He gave us a beautiful world to live in and enjoy. I don't think this is meant to encourage us to act in ways which would harm us or someone else.

I didn't become a new person no one could recognize but I did try to be more careful of what I said, how I acted, being judgmental of others and so on. I also found the pathway we walk with Him isn't always easy. I at least learned to recognize that how I treated others in anger diminished me in my own eyes and in the eyes of those who I lashed out at. But I kept trying.

When your dad was transferred to Kremmling, Colorado we were happy to be closer to our families and in a small town. Bill, you were in kindergarten and Larry, you could roam the neighborhood and make friends with all the neighbors close by. You got to help plant gardens for one family, wash dishes for one lady and we all were doing nicely. We had nothing more serious to worry about than the occasional tooth aches, stomach aches and childhood diseases common in those days. As years went on you both did well in school. We were involved in building a church after years of worshipping in an old warehouse. Friends and family were frequent visitors. We were poor as church mice as the state didn't pay well then and we barely made ends meet some of the time. Dad had many incidents in his job but most local people were understanding and didn't hold it against us if they got a ticket.

He had an ongoing contest with a couple of ranch women he never could catch speeding. It became almost a game with them. In those days the only way to clock a speeder was to use mile markers or other markers he had measured and time how long it took someone to travel from one point to another. Then the speed was determined by simple math. It sounds primitive now and was in comparison to the tools used today. His patrol car had a radio that worked well only in certain spots as hills would cause it to cut out and be useless.

Patrolmen were scarce in rural areas and had to cover for each others days off and vacations. On some days Dad had to cover all of Grand County and parts of adjoining counties. On a winter day when he had been covering an accident in the eastern part of Grand County near Winter Park, he came home to icy, frozen streets in Kremmling. The ice and snow was melting and the water running in the streets in Winter Park and surrounding area, which was said to be the coldest part of the County. He was tempted to transfer to that area as their winters were less harsh than where we lived.

# CHAPTER 4

# *Losing My New Faith*

AT THE TIME THE movie *Camelot* was popular and I felt like we were living in our own version of that life style. Everything seemed to be moving along nicely, we lived close to our families and we had a good life. We were active in community groups and in our church which was growing. Life was good and we were happy.

We lived across the street from the local hospital where I was working as a nurse aide. We were doing well by now, had lots of friends and were enjoying life. Dad's job wasn't too demanding and we both had days off during the week. That would give us time to do special things with you boys such as going fishing or on picnics or other fun things.

It was an early summer day and we had company from out of town. It was our days off so we were visiting and enjoying being at home together with you boys and our visiting family. We had just finished lunch when the phone rang. It was the doctor's office saying someone had reported a state patrolman and others lying on the side of the road just east of town. Dad grabbed his service revolver and drove out to see what was happening. He found his new lieutenant, our county sheriff and a Wildlife Conservation Officer on the ground, all having been shot. An ambulance had followed him and brought in one of the men. People that had come upon the scene offered their help and brought in the other two men. Dad came home to put on his uniform, took his hunting rifle and called a deputy sheriff who lived close by to go with him.

I only can repeat what he told me later. I went to the hospital to help where I could. The ambulance and cars bringing in the wounded officers had to pass our house so I knew the hospital would be busy and I could help.

Your dad had gathered information from one of the wounded and had a description of the shooter's car and the general direction he had taken. Dad drove south of Kremmling to the road leading to the Trough Road. He turned down that road which at that time was just a narrow two- lane dirt and gravel country road. As he rounded a curve he saw a patrolman from Eagle County had set up a road block. That county's deputy sheriff had been badly wounded in a shoot out with the guy Dad was chasing. The shooter abandoned his car which was shot up pretty badly and ran up a hillside into the woods.

Dad got permission from the patrol corporal to go after the killer. He wasn't ever supposed to leave his patrol car unattended without reason and permission. In those days supervisors were more involved in making instantaneous decisions. Dad and his deputy friend went up the hill after the shooter. I heard all this three days later when things calmed down after the shooter was arrested and Dad was home.

Meanwhile when I saw one of the victims was Dad's patrol lieutenant I called the main office in Craig and all afternoon tried to keep them updated on what was happening. The deputy who had been shot at the road block on the Trough was brought in. We all knew his chances were poor. He had been shot in the face and he was losing a lot of blood. Dad's lieutenant and our county sheriff had both been shot in the chest. Neither was bleeding much, outwardly. The lieutenant's aorta had been cut by a bullet. The surgeon found this when he opened up his chest to treat him. The sheriff's heart was contracting as he was shot which caused the bullet to graze his heart sack. Had the heart been expanding it would have been a direct hit to the heart. The Wild Life Officer was shot four or five times but none of the wounds were fatal. The three severely wounded were very quiet, just an occasional groan from one of them. The WCO fellow was more awake and suffering terrible pain.

As the day went on I didn't have time to think about Dad and what might be happening to him until I watched the doctor cut off the lieutenant's uniform so he could treat him. It hit me then that it was the same kind of uniform Dad wore every day and it could have been him lying there. My prayers became more intense for all those on the chase. I had been in a state of shock before this but now I lost all sense of what was going on.

The doctor had removed the lieutenant's Sam Brown belt and holster with the service revolver in it and handed it to me for safekeeping. It couldn't be trusted with a civilian. I was semiofficial by being the wife of an officer I guess. The belt was still warm from his body. That belt and gun were heavy and added to my state of shock. I found a place in a room to wait for someone to come and make some kind of order out of all this for me. I had been going on instinct for some hours and to feel that man's body heat on that belt stopped even that. When Dad's corporal from Craig, ninety miles away, got there I practically threw the gun and belt at him. The lieutenant died later that afternoon. The sheriff's deputy was being moved to Denver and died along the way. Our sheriff survived and eventually recovered in a Denver hospital

After helping with the cleaning up and the men having been sent to Denver or to the morgue, I went home. Our company had left. I think they may have felt to be in the way. I had no idea of where you boys were or what you were doing. I found out later Bill, you were at acolyte training. Larry, you told me you kept walking around our house to try to protect it. It was a day and a half before we saw Dad again when he came in to get his cortisone shot for the arthritis that was starting to cripple him. He said hi and bye and was gone again on the hunt for the shooter. When we talked about it later I told him I had prayed that he would not be the one who found the shooter as he might have to kill him. I knew he would have trouble living with that in later years. Dad told me he had been praying he *would* be the one who found the guy. He was not the one who found the shooter. Make of that what you will.

I have albums with all the newspaper items and

information but at the time I just went through the motions of doing something. Many, many citizens in the county were deputized that day, other officers from all over the state who could be spared from their own duties came and the biggest man hunt in Colorado history took place.

Road blocks were set up all around the area and every car stopped and searched. Railroad trains were stopped and searched as a rail system runs through the area where the shooter was hiding.

When he was finally found and arrested he gave up meekly and was jailed in Hot Sulphur Springs. When our sheriff heard this he asked that the guy be moved to a different area, afraid some of the locals might decide to take the law into their own hands. The shooter was moved to the jail in Craig, Colorado where he stayed until tried, convicted, sentenced to life in prison and moved to Canon City prison. He died there at about age sixty-four. He had escaped once but was found in short order. A lot of us wondered what turned a young man of twenty-four into someone who could so casually shoot those men as they were merely talking to him. His parents said he was a bit of a loner growing up but they too couldn't think why he did this. I don't know if he ever told any one what brought about his actions that day.

I went to his trial and while it was in recess several of us were in the hall talking when he was brought by. As he looked at us I looked into his eyes and saw such deep hatred I had to look away fast.

Since this is part of Grand County's history I am going to add what is called dark humor or a twisted look at the event. The local men had been growing beards for the county fair that fall so some looked like old-time mountain men. The press had a field day with pictures and quotes. Most of those men were game hunters though and knew about handling guns and tracking game. The word was put out on public radio with a description of the fellow being short, pale and very blond. Warnings were posted to not pick up hitchhikers and every town had road blocks at all entrances into town. All cars were stopped and searched. As one car stopped an African American fellow about six foot tall jumped out and yelled I'm not the one you want. He was confronted by many bearded, serious men with big rifles and he wanted to be sure they knew he wasn't the one. The guys laughed later, not at him but just to relieve some of the pressure they were under.

The trains coming out of the area of the search were stopped and every car was carefully searched. In one a hobo was awakened and found he was faced with several rifles with some very serious men behind them. He immediately wet himself then started pleading for his life. It was found he wasn't who they wanted. After they left the train they too laughed to relieve the tension they were under. It sounds cruel now but at that time it helped them keep sane and centered. Almost all knew at least one of the men who had been shot.

It was almost two years before I could go to bed, close my eyes and not see those men bleeding to death and hearing the noise, the smells and relive those hours. I would be able to sleep after I had gone over all the details. I guess that is why even now they are so clear when I have chosen to call them up for this story.

I have included all this though you would rather I hadn't. I want to impress on you that nothing happens that the Lord can't and won't see you through if you ask for help. I also think it so important for young people especially to know what it is really like when someone is shot. Too many today grab a gun and shoot someone without knowing how awful it is to die that way, but also how it is for all the people concerned, family, witnesses and the shooters themselves. Can they ever forget.

I can speak to asking for help or not by my own experience. I chose not to ask for help from anyone and with my great range of anger I told God to shove off. Not a good idea for several reasons. Once I had began to process what had happened I started on God. I had been told He was always there for us, He would keep us safe, on and on for a good long time. In my anger I challenged Him because I had been doing all I was asked to do. We helped build a church, cleaned that church, baked for bake sales to raise money to build that church, been faithful and every argument I could think of. I actually had the nerve to tell Him, if You can't do better than this then leave me alone, I will take care of my family myself, I don't need You, go back to a distant place and I'll call if I ever need You.

Well, that made me into supermom. I was going to control our lives, keep us safe and no one or no thing had better come close again. I was so angry and hurt that I didn't stop to think it was God to whom I was talking. My faith was just beginning to bloom and had been smashed flat in one day!

Two weeks to the day, again on our day off, the four of us had gone to Denver to visit family. On the way home we met the hearse headed to Hot Sulphur Springs where the coronor had his office and mortuary. We wondered who might have died. Only when we stopped at the post office did we find out who it was.

A young man who had caused me many years of worry and concern for my family had died that day. Some years before he had returned home from the service after a stint in Leavenworth prison. He lived with his folks on their ranch outside of town. He had several accidents, minor ones usually, which Dad had to investigate. Any accident victims were taken to the hospital to be checked for injuries. If they had nothing beyond scrapes and bruises the doctor would release them. Dad then had the choice of taking them to jail if they were drunk or taking them home if they were okay. He would use discretion with the locals and if they were just a little tipsy, would take them home to their families. He had done this a few times with this fellow and as a result his parents stopped speaking to us wherever we would meet them on the street or in stores. Their anger at Dad was obvious. They thought he was picking on their son when actually he was trying to save his life.

When his family moved into town they lived on the southeast corner of the block where we lived on the northwest corner. The day I spoke of earlier this young man went into a rage, some said he was psychotic, threatened his parents with butcher knives and jumped through a closed window. His parents called the police. The town marshal responded with his service revolver and his hunting rifle. As they came face to face they were so close the guy cut the end off a finger on the marshal's hand. The marshal shot him with the rifle, causing almost instant death. This took place about half a block from our house. We never knew if he was headed for our home. I couldn't help but wonder 'what if' for a long time.

Some years earlier a well meaning woman had told me that this fellow had made threats against Dad's life and even how his plan was to wait for him and run him off the road some night. Dad just shrugged it off but from that time on I was concerned. If he was late coming home from work or if you boys were late from school my first thought was, does he have them. I was concerned that in his anger at Dad he might take it out on you boys. I never seemed to worry about my own safety, thoughts for the safety of my family was never far from my mind.

When Dad told me who had died I immediately said thank God, he's gone and my family is safe at last. I knew that was wrong and asked God's forgiveness for being happy someone had died. This faith thing was still kind of confusing to me. And when I realized I was talking to God I really got confused about faith all over again. I had told Him to go away and leave me alone and now I was talking to Him again!

## Chapter 5

# *Reality Hidden Again*

Life went on and we tried to get past the ugliness of those awful weeks that scarred us so badly. Not being able to talk about what I was feeling, just stuffing more hate and anger into the mental box of pain brought me to a point where I decided if God couldn't do any better than this I would take over for Him. Have you heard that pride goes before a fall. Well my pride was running the show now. Super mom was born. I would protect my family. I would take care of everything and didn't need to ask God for anything! Wow! I didn't think He was doing a very good job. I didn't think about talking to our priest or someone about what was happening to me. No! I could do this on my own, having always been tough enough to overcome anything!

Within a year I had an emotional breakdown that was devastating. I was afraid of everything again. If someone came to the door and I was alone I would hide. If the phone rang I would cry.

As I sat on the sofa one day in a daze I saw before me an abyss of total blackness. I seemed to know that abyss was complete madness for me. Without thinking, I asked God for help. Just one word! "Help" and the darkness went away. I knew I had come close to losing my mind. Then I finally went to a doctor for help. He gave me one kind of medicine that made me meaner than a two-headed snake. Anyone who talked to me caught hell. So he changed the meds after I told him off a few times.

The new medications helped calm me but I found I had no emotions at all. I just went on living by instinct. I was in this condition for several months, perhaps a year. Oh I was pleasant to everyone after I got over being afraid of them. What false faces we put on when we deal with people. No one had any idea of what I had been through except Dad and he supported me as well as he could. I never stopped believing in God, I just didn't want to have to deal with Him. I kept Him on the shelf I had placed Him on after the horrors of the past year made me mad at Him. We kept going to church for a long time as we thought it best for you boys. When we had a priest that we found to be a false teacher and couldn't in good faith worship with him we quit going to church. That was a good excuse for me to use as I didn't want anything to do with God or Jesus even years later.

In the mean time Dad had to retire from the patrol as his arthritis was so bad he couldn't turn the key to start the engine in his patrol car. I can't remember the exact time I began to feel any emotion. The first one I felt and dealt with was anger and it came back with a vengeance. At times and without warning I would be so angry it overwhelmed me. Of course I wasn't going to tell anyone what was going on. I could handle it like I always did. I had to keep a firm grip on myself when crossed, to not explode into a wild tirade against the person who irritated me. I got lots of practice of anger control over time until other emotions began to counter the anger that had slipped out of the box of pain I lived with. I came to realize that my anger was directed at God and I blamed Him for all the ugliness that had happened, it was His fault that all the awful people had dealt me so much misery.

During those years I started to work as the school superintendent's secretary and also the school district bookkeeper. That was a big help as I had to deal with people all the time. Sometimes it took real control to maintain a pleasant mood when irate parents or students accosted me but I was learning how to do that.

I finally began to see the lame excuses I had used for turning against God instead of looking inside myself for answers. It was a gradual awakening of my soul to the world around me that finally helped me live a reasonably happy life. I don't know just when recovery started, maybe by working at the school and being around the laughing, happy students made it happen. For once I was happy and enjoying life again.

Both of you boys graduated from high school and life had settled into a nice place. We bought a house and remodeled it with help from family and friends. Dad was working by then for the state highway department. His hours were long and so were mine at the school. We were enjoying life and thinking we were okay. We celebrated birthdays, welcomed your wives into the family, enjoyed a lot of holidays and other good times.

As time passed grandbabies started arriving and they certainly caused a lot of excitement at our house. We loved being grandparents and each baby's arrival added to our happiness. However the good times were dampened when I contracted the fatal disease of scleroderma. I have included that story in chapter thirty on miracles, as it is indeed a miracle I am alive today.

## CHAPTER 6

# The True Seed of Faith Grows

ALL THE YEARS GROWING up had to be endured in the best way I could find. I didn't have anyone to confide in, or didn't think I did. The idea of telling anyone what had happened to me was unthinkable. I thought if someone, other than those who had abused me and I knew they wouldn't be bragging about it, that person wouldn't like me and think I was a sinful, terrible person. So I carried my secrets in my box of pain and tried to live like all my friends did. How I envied them their innocence! I had knowledge of things no child should know and that knowledge colored everything in my life. A distorted view of even the most innocent remark or event kept me closely shuttered lest I reveal this nasty knowledge I had. How I lived in fear that someone would find out about all my guilt, real or imagined.

As I became older I managed to tell myself I was safe and relax, no one knew what was going on in my life. Only in middle age was I able to deal with this and simply decide that I was a victim and not guilty of anything. This came about from finding Jesus in my life and knowing that if He accepted me nothing or no one else mattered. He accepted me just as I was, guilt, sin or whatever else I carried all these years. I came to understand that to not accept His forgiveness would say to Him, I am so bad you aren't strong enough to deal with it. That is telling Him you are bigger than He is! If we are ever judged for our life here it will be done by Jesus. The final judgment is His exclusive job.

Jesus talks about the seed being sown on good ground, poor ground and rocky ground. Matthew 13 starting with verse 3 we hear about a fellow planting seed for a crop on different kinds of ground. Rocky ground, dry ground, weed patches and good soil.

He is telling us the seed is our being told about Him and His love for us. The seed on the rocky ground has no chance to take root and grow, which is like our minds that are shut to hearing the good news of His life and death for our salvation. The poor ground is that in which we hear about Him but don't act on it and forget about Him. We don't put down roots and soon we are led to another more exciting place to have fun, or make money or whatever distraction it may be. The world we live in is like weeds that choke out all thoughts of anything except our daily work, fun or anything that keeps us from hearing about Jesus. We don't have time for all this and because we can't see or touch Jesus the time allotted for Him becomes less and less until we just forget about all that and go on to enjoy life as we want to. That is until a crisis comes along and then we begin to remember He has promised to be with us forever.

Now what do we do. Are we embarrassed to ask Him for help because we forgot about Him. Has it been so long since we prayed that we have forgotten how to pray. What other excuse can we use. Perhaps we are strong enough we can handle anything that comes along, making the best of a bad situation. Let me tell you, I tried to handle bad situations by myself and they almost destroyed me. Only by the grace and love of God am I alive, reasonably healthy and able to tell my story. Only when the seeds are sown in fertile ground does anything come of them. Only the good soil provides the nourishment for our souls to grow in Him.

I had thought I was a good Christian who went to church all the time, did everything needed to keep the church clean, tried to spread His word to others. I found I had just scratched the surface of faith. I was living the life of the seed on poor ground that hadn't yet taken root. For many years that seed had somehow survived on rocky soil as my involvement with the Lord was haphazard with long stretches of time between even giving Him much thought.

As I write this, I look back at all the time I wasted that could have been used in much better ways. I didn't have many people who could tell me about the Lord, my friends were as unknowing as I was. So my journey on the path way of life continued in a more secure way but I was still a novice in the faith of following Jesus.

# CHAPTER 7

## *The Dark Side of Life*

AS I WRITE THIS chapter many sad memories come roaring into my mind. The deaths of our loved ones cause us so much grief and heartache it is hard to deliberately call up those times. However, because death is as much a part of us as life I will share my thoughts in a way I hope will be helpful to you when you too have a loved one die.

People shy away from the word die as too harsh to deal with. For me it is an acronym for doorway into eternity. That is where I believe we will be when our earthly bodies die. Our souls are from God and He doesn't let them vanish when our life on this earth ends. Rather our eternal life, our soul, goes on to be with Him wherever that is. I don't know where the heaven we hear of may be but Jesus assured us He has prepared a place for us to join Him when we are through with this state of being that we call life.

What we do not know fills a larger book than what we do know. The many cases of people being resuscitated after dying tells us more about it. Science says this can be accounted for by the brain seeing visions after we die and refuse to believe God can do whatever He chooses. I don't believe everything science tells me as I have lived long enough to see what I was taught when young is no longer true. Things go up and don't have to come down as was once believed, just as the earth isn't flat as ancient people believed. Keep your mind open as there is nothing to fear in accepting God into your life. Rather, it is a comfortable place to be.

Don't ask me why bad things happen to us when we are trying to get by the best way we can. I don't know and no one else does either. This I do know. God doesn't send bad or ugly or sad events to us or into our family's lives. He created us and loves us and would have only happiness and good times for us. He doesn't need to send anything against us. We humans seem to do a good job in self destructive ways without help from Him. We harm our loved ones, our friends and ourselves in so many ways. If from space the world looked like a marble it would be so pitted from bombs and wars it would not be pretty at all.

Sometimes we do what we think is helpful and instead is hurtful. We give answers when we don't understand the questions. We may mean well and seldom would do anything to actually hurt someone by words or actions. Of course there are those who delight in making others miserable. I have had to deal with a few of that kind and have found that they usually act out from their own pain and distress. The theory they might have, I'm sad so it will help if others are sad with me they will feel my pain and sympathize with me. I came to think this was a better way of seeing their action than believing some folks are just ornery and hard to get along with.

A wise story tells us what we can do to help others in this frame of mind. If you find someone down in a well of depression and pain, stopping by and saying I am so sorry is sympathy and doesn't help them more than a few minutes. You can climb down into the well with them and sit and empathize for hours but that doesn't root out their problem. Or you can get a ladder for them to climb out of the well. This is called compassion and is the real help you can give. You can pray with them and if you don't feel qualified to counsel them, take them to someone who knows how to help them deal with their problems. Of course it is always best to ask the Lord to help you help them in the way that is the answer for them. Remember He is the one who ultimately heals us using medicine, doctors, counselors and people who will pray with us.

From my vantage point life is short. When I was a child life seemed to stretch out forever. At times that wasn't a comforting thought. Because of the early years having many mean people as a part of my life, at times a long lifetime was not considered something to work towards.

My first encounter with death happened when at age four, I was playing with a cat that may have been mine or a stray. It either bit or scratched me and of course I yowled and cried. My father, whom I told you of earlier, caught the cat, tied it to the fence and sat me on a step of the porch. He made me watch as he shot and killed it. I don't remember what happened after that, if I was too shocked to cry, to talk about it or what I did. The memory only goes to the point of that black cat jumping high into the air as it died. This is as plain as if etched in a painting. I don't know what the lesson was that he wanted me to learn that day. It seemed to make me very fond of cats and I tried to protect them when I could as I got older. The things that happen to us when we are little kids bend our minds in ways we sometimes don't understand but cause us to act in odd ways.

That was the first experience with death that I can remember. The second was when my mom and I were living with Aunt Myrtle and her son on their little ranch. Some rancher gave me a bum lamb to raise. A bum lamb is one without a living mother to raise it, or I think that is the case. I was five years old and dearly loved that little lamb. First thing every morning I would run out to see him and he would run to me after the first few days. I bottle fed him every day but he wasn't very big.

One morning I ran outside to see my lamb and found him lying dead near a shed. I suppose I cried for a while. I was told he had a disease common to lambs called scours and it is hard to cure them from it. I had watched chickens slaughtered for food and knew cattle died so we could eat but those animals were not personally connected to me like the lamb was. He was mine to care for and I loved him. This hit me hard.

It was about this time I had found a way of dealing with painful events by just shutting them into a secret box that would keep them out of sight and mind. I also had learned not to let other kids see me cry as that empowered them and they would hurt me again. I may have formed this idea by watching adults around me as they went on with their lives without shedding a lot of tears. I suppose they were trying to protect me from whatever sadness they were going through at any time.

As I got older people I knew starting dying and by then I had developed a horror of death that was overwhelming. A few classmates died of diseases for which we now have vaccines but in those years nothing could help them. The first close family member to die was my aunt Myrtle who was the closest to being a grandmother I had. I was twelve and deeply hurt by her death. No one thought to talk to me about death, maybe thinking they were protecting me. I was left to figure it out for my self. That didn't help me with my dealing with losing people or pets. It was just a dreadful mystery that frightened me for years. Only after becoming aware of the Lord and His presence in all things did I come to a place of solace and peace of mind when someone dear to me died.

I had a great fear of being around a dead person. When I worked as an usher in the local theater I had to go backstage to open the two curtains when the movie started. It was dark there and it just happened that the mortuary was right next door to the theater. If I knew someone had died and the body was next door it was all I could do to keep from running down the aisle to get those curtains opened. I then got out of back stage as fast as I could. My chest would tighten and I would have trouble breathing. I was in high school by then and now it seems silly that I had such a reaction but we are programmed early in life to react to things no one explains to us.

It is so sad that those who by their choice or

circumstances are living on the streets in a world that walks by them and doesn't give a second thought to their care or needs. When they die is there anyone to grieve for them. They may have been lost to family for so long no one is aware they have died. Even worse is when a person who has lived among family all his life no one cares enough to shed a tear when he dies. I knew a man who died so unloved by his family because of the way he lived no one cared he was gone. There was no hole left in anyone's heart or life by his death. Perhaps his only monument was an empty space at the dining table.

Where there is life there is death and that is the way of our world. Plants and flowers die when their life span is finished. Animals have a life span that plays out if we don't interfere in some way. I'm not talking about becoming a vegetarian here. Life's rhythms are following a grand plan that we don't understand but the Lord does so I let Him handle it. When a person's life is cut short by whatever means it is much more painful than when a person has lived out his life span and goes through the doorway into the eternal life we are told of in the Bible. This is the goal that is ahead of all of us. As I dealt with the fatal disease I talk about in the chapter on miracles, I came to know this life is not the end of us, just a beginning. Our Lord told us that He was going to prepare a place for us to be with Him. I hold onto that promise and know my body will stop being alive but my soul will go on into that promised place. I will have a new healthy body instead of this old, weary one. Won't that be a great place to be! Of course those of you who don't want to bother with God or Jesus right now have to know that the place I speak of is where they will always be. Do you think you can handle that. So many people today don't want to deal with God as it might interfere with their lifestyle but they all plan on going to heaven when they die. Well that's a conundrum! Be aware that heaven is God's home and our eternal one. Jesus will be hanging around too. Think about it!

## Chapter 8

# *A Parable of Death*

I HAVE GONE BACK into my journals for most of the information I have shared about the sad, bad things in my life. I came across this page written on October 29, 2000. I copy it as I wrote it while dealing with all the recent deaths in the family before that date.

The patio and lawn are covered with the leaves from the cottonwoods. They are a brilliant gold when the sun shines on and through them. Very few bare spots of lawn or cement show through. The ash tree shed its leaves last week, all in a bunch, like a blizzard of brown. The ash tree's leaves turn a beautiful deep russet color before turning brown, but when brown it is only a day or two before all drop. It is as if they can't wait to get this final step over with and the yard is covered with dead brown leaves from just the one tree. The cottonwoods take a while longer and go at a slower pace than the ash. This year they are the prettiest I have seen since we moved here. A few leaves still are on limbs and some will hang on all winter.

As I looked at them I knew that as they age and fall it is their season of death. But such a beauty and solemn stillness comes with their falling and death.

So it is with humankind. We serve out our days, determined by a different clock than the one for leaves on a tree. We are given many more seasons than just one to accomplish whatever it is we would do with our lives. Then it is time for us to fall from the tree of this life. We too have a certain beauty, a sacred silence of God's presence in our death, if we are fortunate. A terrible beauty if you will, nothing kind about it, as struggles too often accompany our dying. Do the leaves on trees also fight to hang on to the limbs. Do they finish their purpose and let go.

As the sun goes down behind the neighbor's roof the brightness has gone from the leaves. The last shine of life grows dull and now gold becomes a yellow turning to brown. The form and bulk is still there but no shine of the living thing is in them.

And so it is with me right now. It seems the shine has gone out of me. Finally I am able, some three or four years later, to allow the deaths of my loved ones to come into my cognizant brain. I am drained, weeping and sorrow filled. Once again, as in years past there were too many, too close together, to be able to grieve each one. My sister Nina's family almost wiped out in two years, only a granddaughter and a great-grandson left. Included in that span of time is the loss of my brother, your uncle Melvin. All died in pain and illness. For them death was surely a welcome release from overwhelming misery and unhappiness. To be brought to such a place from which there was no ease, no comfort and no way to enjoy life anymore was too much to bear. It was hard to watch people who once were so full of life and laughter be brought to a place of being incapable of caring for themselves and no longer able to enjoy life in any way. For those of us left, it is true we can understand their need to be done with it at last, but it leaves such a hole in our hearts and lives.

Along with family members I have had many close, dear friends die in the past few years. There seems to be no order to the causes, no respect for age or position in life. Nothing that can tell me what I would like to know. And I suppose it is none of my business. God's plan works one way and we people seem to work our own way and the two don't always coincide for a good outcome. I am assured though that when we die all is well with us. God's plan then takes over and we can't mess it up any more with our knowing what is best.

# Chapter 9

## Seeking Peace and Finding

Since writing the last pages of 2000 I am now back in present time. Looking back lets me see so many more deaths of loved ones. Being so much younger than my siblings, I grew up with my nieces and nephews who are just a few years younger than me, the closest being four years younger and on down the line from there. There were four nieces and three nephews once. Now only two nieces and one nephew survive. I also claim their spouses as my family which adds four more people to the count. It has been like losing siblings all over again. And then I also am the only one still alive from my generation, all siblings and their mates are gone now. It is a lonely feeling but they all were so ill that I can't wish them back. My mother and step-father, your Grandma Lou and Papa Bill and my father and step-mother died many years ago. Dad's mother, your grandma Dorothy and his step-father Papa Leonard died years ago too. All suffered from various illnesses and were happy to be out of this life, with the exception of Papa Leonard who died suddenly of a heart attack at an earlier age.

Life doesn't pay much attention to our wishes and desires when it comes to health issues and death. There are scarcely enough words to comfort us during the loss of a loved one. But being assured that this life isn't the end but rather just the beginning helps ease the sorrow a little bit. That is why I tell you my story, to let you know from my own experiences that life does go on.

Several books are available that were written by people, especially little kids, who have gone on and came back to tell about it. I suggest you read "90 Minutes in Heaven", "Heaven is for Real" and "Trevor's Song" to hear what they have to say. They aren't filled with a lot of fancy theology and big words, just a simple story of what they experienced and saw.

What happened to your dad will let you know that we all, not just a chosen few, are special to the Lord and He is with us through all things, including our dying. Not everyone has the same type of experience. We each, being individuals, have conditions that are special to us rather than everything being like it was stamped out of a mold for all. Our comfort, our reassurances are unique to us but at the same time close enough to everyone's that we can see the Lord's gift in all of them.

After years of battling health problems your dad was slowly becoming more disabled and uncomfortable. You watched as this happened but I tell it here for the sake of my story to make sense. I tell you in chapter thirty four the details of my being called to a healing ministry. Dad always was involved in that ministry, usually closing his eyes and praying for protection from any evil that may be visiting during our prayer sessions. This is necessary as evil does exist and is waiting for us to be involved in deep prayer for others so it can come into the group. That was Dad's part of the ministry and he was faithful in it.

One evening he had asked for prayers for himself. He was feeling doubt about being good enough to be in God's grace. Did he know his time was growing short. He had never asked for this type of prayer before.

This happens to most of us at one time or another as we look at who we are and wonder how we can be worthy of God's love and grace. Don't think doubting God's existence or thinking that Jesus isn't real is bad. A priest told us doubt isn't a sin, apathy is. Apathy is not caring one way or another. Doubt is just asking questions for which we would like answers. We doubt ourselves and that is just being truly honest with ourselves. We have God's assurance that His grace is always with us and is sufficient enough for us even in our weakest moments.

After the group prayed that the Lord would give him assurance that he was firmly in His grace, Dad took his place behind me. I always sit facing the person I pray for and hold their hands. After anointing with holy oil the one we will pray for I begin to pray for what their needs are. As I prayed with a woman, Dad with eyes closed and arms stretched out to encompass the group, was praying the prayer of protection. He said that for some reason he opened his eyes which he never had done before. Just above my wrist and hand were the words I Love You in block letters about an inch high. So he quickly closed his eyes! But curiosity got the better of him and he opened his eyes again. The words were still there. He didn't say anything to the rest of the group at the time and went on with his prayers.

On the way home, just the two of us in the car, he told me about his experience. He didn't know what to make of it and said he thought it was something I had done. I laughed and told him I could do some things but this wasn't one of by any means. I then asked him to repeat it. When he did I finally was able to convince him that he had received a personal message from the Lord in answer to our prayers. No one else in the group saw this. It was for him alone. He was to know from the Lord that he was in God's grace and not to be concerned about it. That's a neat way to get a message! It has never happened to me or others I have told about it. It may have been necessary for him to see those words in block letters, he kept emphasizing block letters, for him to accept this message. Had he heard the words he may have thought he was hearing things. He was a bit of a skeptic about that and might not have believed it.

After the emergency surgery from which he never fully recovered he spent many days in pain and misery. But he seemed to stay in a place of acceptance of it all. Two days before he died he told me he didn't think he was going to make it through this episode of sickness. That scared me and I immediately started trying to talk around it, saying we would take it a day, an hour, a minute if necessary, at a time. I so wish now I had let him tell me if he had received a word from the Lord to make him aware that time was short. Instead I tried to hide my fear of what might be coming.

When a people die at home it is the law that they be taken to a hospital or morgue where a coroner can do the official stuff that is necessary to determine cause of death. Dad's heart specialist was on duty in the ER that day and knowing Dad's heart history, said there was no need to do an autopsy. That was a blessing. When the nurses brought Dad into the private room where we all were gathered so we could say goodbye before the mortuary came, I was given another gift. He was seventy four years old and looked every day of it before he died. When he was wheeled into the room I was amazed. I saw a man about twenty five years old, wonderfully healthy looking with a faint golden tone to his skin.

I asked our priest how she saw him and she said he just looked at peace. I have never asked my family members who were there, I don't know why. At the mortuary of course he looked like he had when he died. Nothing like the loved one I saw at the hospital. I choose to think I was allowed to see him in his newly perfected state as he is now, in heaven. That picture in my mind is the one I still see. What a comfort it is.

I have since talked with people who have seen this same glow about their loved ones either before they die or soon afterward. I assume this is a gift from the Lord to assure us that our loved one is home safely with Him.

Light in itself is invisible. We see it only when it reflects off something. I believe that the golden glow on Dad was the reflected light of a heavenly being, perhaps the Lord Himself, present with him as he died, come to take him home.

## Chapter 10

# A Time of Death

It was Thanksgiving morning 2004 that your dad died. After eating breakfast with us he went into the small bedroom to watch a football game. I wasn't aware that anything was happening until one of the family came to the kitchen where we were preparing the turkey for dinner. He said his grandpa was having trouble and I should come with him which I did.

As I look back it seemed the day just evolved slowly into the nightmare it was to become. After the ambulance came the EMTs worked on Dad on a gurney for the required time before taking him to the hospital. .

It seemed even the weather was against us as when the time came for his memorial service and burial. The roads were impassable as a blizzard condition existed in some parts of the country. This prevented a lot of people from getting here including the priest who was to do the homily, who was a friend of Dad's. We reversed the procedure of the day, going to the cemetery first, then to the service at church. As we were sitting in the car at the cemetery waiting for the people to lead us to the grave site I was suddenly able to tell God how angry I was.

This hadn't happened until now but dealing with such a nasty, snowy day freed me to be honest with Him. I dared say, I know you didn't cause this to happen but because you allowed it to happen the least you can do is make it stop snowing long enough for us to get this burial service finished. I was able to be completely honest with God and dared to let Him know how I felt. I said this quietly so others in the car would not hear. Just before the procession to the grave began, the sky overhead cleared, the sun shone on us and the snow stopped. It was really cold but clear during the burial service. As soon as we got back to the cars the sky closed over, snow began to fall and we drove to the church. A little girl had stayed in the car because of the cold. She told me that she had seen a rainbow over us all at the grave. She was five years old and I don't think she would be able to make that up. Only after all was done and we were back home did we begin to see God's hand in our day, the sky clearing just over us long enough for the service and then beginning to snow again, the girl seeing the rainbow. When we got to the church there was a crowd of family and friends who were such a comfort and the priest led a meaningful service in Dad's memory.

Only your dad and I knew about the ritual we had with pennies. In the 1970's the government had been talking about not making them any more so I had started saving them. Dad saved all his pennies for me. He would empty his pocket and put them on the dresser until he thought there was enough to bother with. Then, instead of putting them in the quart jar I kept them in until I rolled them in tubes, he would put them on my bedside table. I then would put them in the jar for later. We laughed about this way of doing things but never changed over many years.

A few weeks after he died I was making my bed when a wall light came on. Now this light is one that you have to touch to turn on, it takes three touches to bring it to full brightness and a fourth touch turns it off. When it came on it startled me a bit but I was still in shock and didn't pay much attention to it. When I walked near it to leave the room I touched it to turn it off. That was the fourth touch. Then I realized someone or something had turned on that light, not me. Another day I found three pennies on my dresser arranged like a clover leaf.

For some reason I had not gone downstairs to the TV room and where my album cropping table sits. I don't know why I went down there on this day. In the TV room in front of the futon I found three pennies in a straight line, about six inches apart. This did startle me. I asked all the family if they had done this and no one had. I don't understand what happened or why it happened or who did what each time. I felt a sense of comfort and peace because of it though. After all this time I still can't explain or understand it. Was I being let know that all was well with dad. That may be the only answer to these strange events.

As I was sitting drinking a cup of hot chocolate the day I was writing this page, I realized I have never really dealt with the death of your dad in my innermost heart and soul. I began to truly know how great my loss was. As tears long unshed started, I began to feel the deep sadness which has been my constant companion since that day. I have been able to function daily and enjoy life to a degree but never fully because he has not been here to share that enjoyment with me.

I still sleep in the same bed as before, I sit in the same pew in church as before, but I now sit at the table across from where he sat rather than next to where he used to sit.

All our married lives we sat next to each other at the table when alone, for meals or just talking. I don't know when or why I moved but now I look across to where he should be and try to imagine I can see him there. Just once more God, is what I ask, knowing that once more would not be enough and would just open the door to ask again. It is not given to me so I look into the memories of our times together and cry. Don't get me wrong. This doesn't happen often thankfully, or I would begin to lose the strength to go on.

Most of these times are triggered by a song I'm listening to or something I'm reading. They don't last long as I won't let that pain control me.

The day my hon died my brain, as usual when handed something too painful to cope with, shut down. A doctor once told me that's nature's way of saving our sanity.

I don't know if that is so but it happened that day and continued for a long time. I still acted as normally as possible to spare those around me from watching me grieve and feeling they had to comfort me. I still had to breathe, to get out of bed to ease the pain of arthritis. That disease was a blessing for once and kept me from giving up and staying in bed, hiding from the truth. Only when I slowly began to allow the truth to filter into the open did I find how completely devastated I was. My life revolved around him. This wasn't supposed to happen. Who was I without him to hear my ideas, share happiness and sadness with, the only one who truly understood me and knew my story. I simply didn't care if I lived or died. I found it to be true that when you marry you become as one and part of me had died with him. Once again the Lord had to come to my rescue, protect my soul, lift my eyes to a world that went on with or without me. After a little over a year I was able to begin to live for the sake of living, not acting by reflex alone.

I wrote a poem when a friend's husband died and I tried to imagine what that might be like for her. When we write poetry we often can reach a depth of understanding that is not possible in other ways. Little did I know how true the words of this poem were when I wrote. The poem is in the poetry section of this book.

I can't understand why it is that I, supposed to die many years ago, am still here and have seen so many of my loved ones make that step through the doorway into eternal life. I no longer fight against it by looking for cause, or blaming or crying out for an answer. I know God's plan for our universe is so far beyond my comprehension it is foolish to ask. If He were to tell me could I grasp what I heard. Would I have the foggiest idea. I don't think so. I only know I trust that He still loves all of us, cares about us and possibly wonders if we will ever learn what He would have us learn, to stop destroying each other and ourselves in so many ways, from the smallest harsh word to the biggest battle field! To understand that He created our universe, that all of creation is dear to Him, not just me or you because we are such nice kids!

I struggle to find words to tell you how much better life is when we include the Lord. I don't have to worry about things that used to take up my time trying to control or change in some way. It is such a comfort to be able to pray for somebody or something and know that my prayers are heard. The answer might not be the way I would have done it, imagine that, but it is proven that His way is better in the long run. C.S. Lewis says it best, "if God were to give us what we ask for it may have been fatal to us. We can't see the big picture but He can".

# CHAPTER 11

## A Loss Too Deep to Acknowledge

THIS CHAPTER IS HARD to write and may be hard for you to read but it is necessary in explaining my journey with the Lord. I have chosen to put this at the end of the chapters on life and death, although sad in itself, tells us that there is so much more than we know or understand now. It gives us the knowledge that God's plan is in place and working. No one knows how many days we have to live on this earth. Only God knows that. Some feel God has assigned us a certain number of days to live, based on Psalm 139 and other writings. Read the Psalm to find where this thought comes from.

I don't know if this is true or not. Only God knows what His ways are and what His plan for us can be. Because Jesus lived fully as a human being, was scourged and crucified on the cross, He knows what death is and the heartache and loss we go through. The promise He made is that we too shall be with Him in a place He has prepared for us when it is our time to leave this earth. His sacrifice that day so long ago cost Him dearly but gives us the gift of life when our time comes to die.

I talked a little about the death of loved ones or pets but I feel it is best to tell about the time when death became very close and personal in such a way that my life was changed. At first the change was subtle. I didn't understand what was happening until a class lesson brought out a painful time in my life that I had hidden from my thoughts as too awful to deal with. By now I was becoming an expert on stuffing heart aches and misery into that mental box of pain and could do it without a lot of intentional thought.

When you were about a year and a half old, Bill, I became pregnant again. This was during a recession that had hit us hard and we were struggling to get by but we didn't think it a bad thing to have another child. At about two months into the pregnancy, I had a miscarriage. I don't know the medical term for it but the placenta separated from the uterine wall.

The older women in our families told me not to grieve, that this was God's way of correcting a mistake, the baby would have been malformed, we already had one child and that was enough, and on and on. Being young and still believing what older folks told me I just buried my sorrow and grief and went on with life.

Some time later we had you Larry, and happily settled for our two sons. I don't remember dwelling on the loss of the second child but probably mentioned it at times when women got together and discussed their pregnancies as younger women are prone to do.

Some years later when visiting with a friend, she mentioned she had been in the lab of the doctor who had delivered both of you boys. He took care of me during the loss of our other baby. She said the doctor had a bottle on a shelf that had a label on it that said Blandford baby. My baby was in a bottle on a shelf. It was like a hard slap to my head and heart to hear that and I was instantly angry at the doctor. But once again I swallowed my rage at the doctor, my heartache and forgot about it. Into the box of pain it went.

Many years later in a spiritual development class we were asked one week to compare how we were all alike. The next week we were asked to find out how we were completely different from others in the class. The first thing that came to my mind was that I hadn't heard any women say they had suffered a miscarriage. I stopped that thought as being too painful to discuss. I came up with another something for the class that seemed to answer the question.

Later that night as I was lying in bed trying to say my nightly prayers I found my mind was scrambled so badly I couldn't concentrate enough to pray for anyone. I asked God what was going on, what was the matter with me. This was one time I heard that small, still voice of the Lord! I felt like I was enclosed in a capsule of total silence and peace, not an out-of-body type of thing but rather isolation from the world. I was in bed and fully awake. The voice said, why do you pray for two children when you have three.

Being stunned for a time before I was able to think or say anything I finally said, how will you know who I am praying for. My baby didn't have a name. The gentle voice said, call him Israel. Then everything returned to normal. I was once again lying in bed and praying, this time praying for three sons. I still pray for the three.

The next day I was unable to understand what had happened so I made an appointment to talk to our priest. It took two tries to get to the church because I was reluctant to discuss this with anyone. I called and cancelled the appointment with the priest and then knew I had to go talk to him so I called back and told him I would be right there. Father John, after hearing my story of the night before, suggested a healing of memories rite and we called your dad to come to be with me. It was terribly painful as I mentally relived all those days when I should have acknowledged my baby but didn't, just putting my grief into my mental box of pain and slamming the lid down again. But this time I saw Jesus holding my hand and comforting me as I walked through the entire time of loss. I cried for a long time, finally shedding the tears I should have cried when my baby died. I grieved for several years and as I write this tears are falling again. Death became very personal and very close now. I finally knew I had a third child that I had never held or seen but in some way loved as if I had held him.

Don't ever believe that a baby isn't alive and in God's hands during the pregnancy until the delivery. A friend of mine believed a child didn't become real or have a soul until he or she was born. Don't be afraid to grieve for those lost children you have never seen or held. They are safe in the Lord's care and I believe one day I will see my third son as he was meant to be. I know this because the voice of the Lord told me his name and so I know he is alive and well. I suppose there will be some who say I imagined this but I again tell you I don't have the ability to imagine the unexplainable nor would I do so if I could. This is too serious to play games with. I also now know why I am against abortions.

# CHAPTER 12

# *Loss of Respect for Life*

KNOWING NOW THAT LIFE is sacred from conception I also realize that the world does not see that to be true. I recall a cynical joke from some years back: a couple surrounded by a bunch of kids, the father remarks, we don't necessarily like kids, they are just a by-product of what we do like.

I have known women who are at the mercy of their husbands' demands even if a dozen or more pregnancies occur. The time has come for men to be held responsible for raising all the children they help create. Women need to take control of their lives and demand that care be taken so pregnancy does not happen unless wanted. If I had my way laws would be passed causing this to be so with rather dreadful punishments if not taken seriously. For men who spread their sperm around like they were planting corn with no intention of taking responsibility for the child conceived, I think sterilization is the answer, married and single men both. Women who try to have children to trap a man into marriage or to get more government monies should be sterilized after first request for an abortion. This sounds harsh and is but it will stop many unwanted children being born and then abused or killed when they get in someone's way. The death rate for children who are killed by abusive adults is horrific and must be stopped.

Having children is not a right but a privilege and should be held as a sacred trust. A time when the population of the earth was sparse an excuse could be made for many babies being born. The world is fast becoming over populated and will soon overwhelm resources to feed even the best of us. In today's world it has become a horrible truth that our children are considered expendable by too many.

In the 1960s a team of college students in the state of New York did an experiment. A comfortable living space with plenty of food and water was created for a pair of mice. Being the nature of mice to breed rapidly within a short period of time the space became more crowded, the food was running out and water was not available at times. As the situation became worse the adults started killing their young so they could survive.

Today that seems to be the answer to conditions that people find themselves in without understanding what they are doing. Some don't understand how fragile a baby is and use physical means to make them stop crying or whatever it is that annoys the adult. Such means would hurt an adult. Older children are abused in ways that are beyond me as to how people can even think of such evil things to do.

Why and how has this happened. One reason is that life is no longer considered sacred. Children that are badly abused physically and mentally live a life that is horrible.

They have a distorted view of life because of the abuse they suffered. God has no place in the lives of the people who harm others so easily to further their own needs. If He has ever been introduced to them they choose to disregard any thought of Him or His plan for them. They live in the moment without thought of tomorrow, only today and satisfying their wants as they see them portrayed in movies and TV, advertising for more and more things.

If the media thinks I blame them they are right. Some of the writers and actors have lowered the human being into something lower than four legged animals and consider it funny. What was once a wonderful gift of love for another person has been turned into a mockery, a dance of destruction that lasts for a night, an hour, a year or whenever boredom sets in and causes a separation. Entertainers in movies, television or live shows promote false ideas that to be happy we need lots of stuff, money, big everything to outdo the rest of the world. That is hooey and they know it! But it makes them money so they can have more of everything.

During the 1960's and 70's too many entertainers were involved in a drug world and the fantasies they enjoyed showed up in their work. It led a young generation into the false idea of what was real. My generation raised our kids during this time and tried to protect them from the lies but too many times did not succeed in this effort. It is handed down to my grandchildren's generation and will go on into the next. The sports figures who were supposed to be models for our young people have fallen into the trap of do anything to win. New motto: cheat to win!

This is done for money and fame. Do those folks think they can buy their way into heaven or talk their way into God's presence when they die. I don't know if they can plead their case eloquently enough. They need to own up to what they have done and make peace with the Lord and those they have misled. Do they worship any god inside their lives. Do they know that He has promised forgiveness when asked for.

When Jesus forgave people their sins He also said "go and sin no more", not go ahead on and live like you have been. How many confessions are acceptable to Him. How does He see our behavior continuing in what He has forgiven. Is there a lesson somewhere in that. Do you wonder if He maybe thinks, not him or her again with same thing. When will they ever learn, as the song Where Have All the Flower Gone asks. I don't have the answers, just the questions.

# Chapter 13

## The Desert of Despair

Many people, better educated and perhaps closer to God than I, have written about being in a desert of despair. The desert of pain, grief and loneliness with little relief. Some become deeply depressed and see no way out of their despair. It is a harsh, hard place to be, a place no one can come into to comfort you as it is all mental and spiritual. Today there are medications given to repair the depression but medicine can't heal it completely unless the cause is a physical or chemical problem in our bodies or brains. Medications only put a band-aid on a spiritual desert, making us feel good but still deeply wounded and not knowing why. The Lord, if allowed, can and will come in and sit with you. He will help you identify your pain and heal it for you. However you have to invite Him into your desert place.

I have walked different deserts a few times—some with sand, cactus, thorns and dullness. Others haven't even had the break of cactus, only the dull, dry sand of pain so deep

I can't touch it. Brought to that place by the death of a loved one, betrayal by a trusted friend, ugly events that cloud my mind against anything nice or beautiful. With a deep need to rest in my darkness without allowing it to overwhelm me I resist dealing with it and run away, doing, going, being, anything to keep away from the darkness. It makes me uncomfortable to see myself grieve, never mind letting others see me so. Does this go back to learning to never cry in front of others.

If it is true that depression is caused by repressed anger I found one cause of a trip to the desert as I had a lot to be angry about. Of course that really helps us to get better! Nursing anger just cuts deeper and deeper into your heart and soul.

Repressed grief can cause a walk through the desert of depression and sorrow pondering what might have been, if only. What would make a difference. Dealing with the hidden anger between siblings brought on by their hard, young years caused me sorrow that I had to keep hidden or it would have pulled me into their story. I didn't have to suffer through that story with them, thank the Lord. All I could do was to understand why they acted as they did towards each other and love all of them in spite of it. Their anger only lashed out at me once in a while and only for short times.

Only when, once again, I ask for help from the Lord and it comes does the grayness and sadness start to lift. The cause is identified, prayers for strength to overcome it, asking help to forgive the betrayer, prayers to work through and accept the grief lets the healing begin. I learn that bad or evil is in this world and can only touch me as much as I allow it to. Then I can begin to walk out of the desert toward a bluer sky, a greener earth and a healing of spirit and heart.

I have found that in these desert places I have the chance to grow closer to the Lord, to strengthen my relationship with Him. The bad days have helped make me who I am, have helped me become the person I am now, and hopefully becoming the person God would have me be.

Hard times make us strong by showing us we are able to overcome them with help the Lord promises He will give us. The good days are gifts to be enjoyed because of who I am, molded and shaped to see the reality of God's world as it was created and to stand in awe of it and Him. We are able to overcome the bad times to a degree by our own doing. It is never as complete as it is when the Lord helps with overcoming them.

There have been times when a little help would have been appreciated and didn't seem to happen. People live through heartbreak and tragedies all the time. Does praying for help bring it. Not necessarily as we ask for it, rather it comes as what we need at that moment. That makes some say He doesn't answer our prayers. He does but He knows what is best for us and gives us that which will comfort and strength us in the best way at that particular time. When we look back over time we understand how His wisdom is better than our wanting.

Not understanding this much earlier in life has caused me to have to undergo some terribly painful times and way too many trips to the desert. God does not send the bad times to us or in any way hurts us. In Matthew 5: 45 we hear that God's sun rises on the good and the bad, the rain falls on all people alike, whether they are holy or evil.

We know good things happen to bad people. Some live sumptuous lives by cheating and stealing from others. Those people have to answer to our laws but will answer to God someday. I don't have to try to figure out why life happens this way. I am glad I don't. We would all like to see justice done on behalf of those cheated or injured by these people. Some one said you may be forgiven in heaven but pay the consequences of your actions here on earth. That would be fitting when and if it happens.

God is a loving, merciful God. He would like to see all of us, young or old, male or female, happy in a perfect world He created for us. We harm ourselves and others enough. Why would He want to give us more pain or trouble. He must be a loving and caring God or He would have thrown up His hands long ago and said the time has come to end it.

Trips to the desert of desolation come about by not dealing honestly with things that wound us deeply, causing us pain we won't or can't deal with at the time they happen. Healing and being able to see the way out of that desert comes when we look at each event with honest eyes, decide to forgive and go on with our lives. Until we do, whatever has caused the deep hurt is still in control of us and makes us miserable.

This is not easy to do. It hurts all over again just like it hurt when we were first wounded, but it only lasts a brief time as we begin to see how we have allowed it to control us. At last, as we see it clearly and objectively, we can get on with forgiving what or who has caused it. This is easier if we ask the Lord for help.

To try to brush off these deep feelings is trying to run from them, hide from the hurt, seal them off without knowing that we are letting them be seared into our heart and soul. When I failed to go through a period of honest grief for my child lost through miscarriage I set myself up for several years of mild depression that I didn't recognize until I wrote about it. I had put on a false face that let people think I was enjoying life. I was only living on the surface. I see it now. Until the class that brought it to mind I had buried the heartache so deeply I had forgotten about it. It is said that the worst heartache and grief a person can have is to lose a child to death. It must apply even to the unborn children, though perhaps not as intensely as when a child who lived and was part of the family dies.

We all take journeys through the desert places that color our view of life. We make the decision to work to get out of the desert or linger there. I have known some people who simply were too worn out to even try to let their pain go, having struggled with it for such a long time. Or after a time they began to be comfortable with the sympathy and care it brought from other people. I also know from my own experience that we can be unaware that we are depressed because we continue to go about life and think we are okay. One clue to consider is a fast, angry reaction to things that shouldn't bother us that much. It can be a door that I seem to always run into, a cupboard door I hit my head on because I didn't close it, a car that pulls out in front of us so we have to slow down. Consider what makes you angry and why.

We are told that depression is the result of suppressed

anger! If that is so I can understand why I had periods of unreasonable anger at times. Anger at God! Wow, do we dare the lightening strike. I assure you if that were a possibility I would have been struck several times and be nothing but a charred cinder by now. Nothing we can think of will cause Him to retaliate. We should be eternally thankful for that being true. Remember, Jesus lived through life as a human. He knows well what we deal with. It may not be exactly the same but we don't seem to invent anything that is too new no matter how hard we try. He saw what people around Him dealt with daily, in a world harsher in many ways than our world today. So He knows!

One problem we have is thinking depression is something to be ashamed of. There is such an aversion to anything seen as dealing with the brain not functioning properly that it is better to hide that we are depressed and sad. Good grief, where does such nonsense come from. Those who have never had to deal with being broken by life!

In the book of Ecclesiastes' first chapter we are told that there is nothing new in the world, what is being done now has been done many times, in many different ways probably but the root action is the same no matter the year, century, or people doing it. We mere mortals can put a new twist on an old action but it all ends up being the same thing.

What appears as new to us in the physical world, such as quasars, worm holes and the like have always been here, taking time and intelligence to find them. Science continues to prove that what is now has always been but has yet to prove that matter can create itself out of nothing.

I would like to know what they think went bang and where it came from before it went bang.

I cite a story to prove science still has a ways to go to outdo God: One day a proud scientist approached and told Him, saying we have finally found the way to create life. We are now as smart as you! We are now as great as you! God looked at the scientist and told him to show what he could do. The scientist reached down and grabbed a handful of dirt. God said, “oh no, get your own dirt”. The scientist, head down, walked away.

I am not putting science down in any way as I recognize the great contributions it has made and continues in make our world. The advances in medicine, the ease of our life styles as opposed to a hundred years ago, and in so many other ways need to be acknowledged and thanks given for those contributions. If not for science we would still be dealing with many more deadly diseases than we have today along with primitive ways of daily life. We have better food, clean water, great ways to travel, and so many, many more things to be grateful for. I have a glass top cook stove thanks to the tiles made for the space shuttles. No more hours spent cleaning gas or electric stoves with so many parts and pieces!

Does this help you to know that what you have gone through has happened many times before, in different times to other people. If you were to read a good history of the human race you would see that the method used today to damage others, physically, mentally or emotionally has all been done before. Nothing new under the sun indeed!

# Chapter 14

# Acting as Judge and Jury

I HAVE STRUGGLED WITH how best to write on emotions, in separate chapters for each one, sub title them in one chapter, or how best to categorize them. I chose to put each in a separate chapter and overlap on some.

I am not an expert on these topics but have managed through my life to recognize what each means to me and the wide space that separates them. In this wide space are the trips to the mountain top in joy and beauty and the trips to the valley of despair, pain and hatred for someone or something. I can only write about my own experiences. I have learned with the help of many people either through talking it out or reading books by people who have walked their path before me, sharing how to cope with like happenings.

The biggest and best help has come through praying about each incident or event and having the Lord show me how to find answers, to even hear His voice at times. The Bible is a great source for answers and in the searching I find ways to enjoy the blessing and help to overcome the bad feelings I have toward others. Much work, prayer and reading has shown me the way to forgive. It has taught me how to let go of the power bad things have had over me and to hear what the Lord would have me do.

I spent many years going along thinking I was okay and doing fine considering what I had been through. It is so easy to fool ourselves into saying, I'm okay—you're okay, when the truth is we are not okay.

Years ago a teaching of this way of thinking was going around to offset the narrow, judgmental attitudes of a lot of religious people. Narrow, sometimes mean spirited thinking had turned so many people against anything to do with the Lord or His teachings that a new idea of you are okay came in to let people know they weren't completely lost in the Lord's eyes. It didn't go quite far enough to explain that the Lord is the one we answer to ultimately, not our neighbors who look down on us because we don't walk in lock step with them. I am glad if I am to be judged it will be by Jesus, not righteous people who seem to think He needs their help in that job. Now don't think for a minute that I haven't been guilty of doing my share of judging in past years. It took some hard lessons to get beyond that stage of my life, to see the truth in myself, that my behavior, while maybe different from others, was still not close to being saintly enough to be judge and jury against other people.

We all need to use judgments in our lives, but not on other people. Judgment is the capacity to make reasonable decisions, especially in regard to the practical affairs of our life. It can be described as good sense and wisdom. We must look at everything with discerning and judging, not judgmental, eyes to keep us out of trouble in this world, to be able to make smart decisions for our well being. We can determine if the action we are considering taking is good for us or will be bad for us or others. Undetermined rash action usually leads to someone getting wounded, physically, mentally or emotionally. Even our words can do so much damage to people when we say things to get even for a hurt done to us or just because we are having a bad day.

Some words leave deep scars on our hearts and the one saying them may never know how much we have been hurt. You don't hear the book of James quoted too often maybe because it has some tough things to listen to. James writes in chapter 3 about our tongues. Doesn't that sound exciting! Well it is when James tells us that although the tongue is only a small part of our body it is the most dangerous. Our tongue is the one part of us that can't be tamed although we can tame wild lions and tigers and other vicious animals. It is like a small fire that can set a huge forest ablaze with just a few words and can cause more harm than we can dream of. We can destroy people with a few words spoken.

That is powerful condemnation of how we speak against others. When we don't know their circumstances or care to hear their stories, afraid we might have to change our minds and help them rather than condemn them, we let our tongues run wild!

A quote from an American Indian saying: do not judge another man until you have walked a mile in his moccasins.

Some people don't care about this. This is for you to decide. Do you react or not. Do you pass on the hurt to someone else with hurtful words or actions, which will be what you will answer for when Jesus asks you His questions. Or do you grit your teeth and work on forgiving that person who hurt you.

Their actions are theirs, theirs to answer for someday. Your reaction is yours and you decide what it will be. That is what you have to concern yourself with. Now we get to the forgiving part. Before we do that we need to look at the emotions we live with.

# CHAPTER 15

## *Love*

THERE ARE FOUR KINDS of love according to those who know these things. The first love we are aware of is storge, the love parents have for their child and what the child has for parents. The second love is philia for brotherly or sisterly love we feel between siblings, other relatives or even close friends. The third love is eros which is erotic or romantic love. The fourth love is agape which is the love God has for us.

All four loves are what we feel emotionally and cause us to act in kindness and caring for those we love. Each has to be handled gently and needs constant attention to survive. Any love will die eventually if not nurtured and fed just as our physical bodies need to be nurtured and fed to survive. In the world of constant demands on our time and thoughts it is easy to forget this and assume everything is okay just as it has always been. Sometimes we don't realize things have changed until the train wreck happens and we can't figure out what we do next to get back to the way things were. It is easier to keep the train on the track than to try to put it back on after the wreck. For instance, when a marriage moves toward divorce we need help to put it back together and it takes a lot of effort to bring it back where we would like it to be. That effort may be painful but not as painful as losing a loved one to divorce.

Relatives or friends may leave and never be a part of our lives again. Because of problems that come up between us are not worked out before too much hurt occurs, a relationship can be ruined and we lose someone dear to us. We all have to contribute love and care to the relationship, be it marriage, friendship, siblings or extended families. Knowing there are some who are self centered enough they can suck the life out of a relationship puts us in the position of trying to overcome their harm as gently as possible when you care enough to keep that relationship in your life.

Sometimes I had to get pretty vocal with my siblings to put things right. Sorry to say that would only hold for a time until something else would start their nitpicking again. That came from years of nurturing the abuse they had suffered growing up that caused deep anger towards each other. Each believed they had suffered more abuse than the others and that caused a gulf between them. I think they were never able to overcome that gulf. One of them finally realized that the past was done and couldn't be undone and learned to enjoy life. The other two carried deep scars that were partially healed but always stood between them having a good relationship. The idea of forgiving each other and getting on with life never seemed to appeal to them.

This made family gatherings interesting at best and hard to get through at worst.

One of the ways your dad and I would get through tough times of pressure, worry and cares was to look back to the times we were courting, a word that has been out of use for a long time. We would remember those first years we were so in love and so happy. By concentrating on those times we could put the present worry or care into perspective and get through it, still in love and happy with each other. Even my siblings, Dad didn't have any, would cause me to have to think really hard about the happy times we had together when one of them would do something that irritated me. I even dared getting mad enough at God to tell Him to go away and leave me alone. It took some time to get back to being able to remember the times He had been at my side and loved me through stupid or threatening days. This is all easy to sit here and write. Let me tell you, the doing isn't nearly that easy but it gets easier with practice. Life seems to give us lots of times to practice though.

## Chapter 16

# *Hate*

I have sat here for a time reading all the material I have at hand, trying to come up with a good definition of hate. I know how it feels, know how it acts, but not sure how to describe it. I learned some of things that cause it at an early age. It covers a lot of ground. I finally went to the dictionary: intense dislike or aversion to something. Hatred is intense hate.

Some of the feelings coming from hate or hatred are the desire for revenge, bitterness and rage. I guess at one time or another I have felt all of these when hurt so badly that nothing could ease my pain and sorrow. Revenge is to want to get even on the same scale as the hurt experienced. This can be such a destructive emotion. I have watched a family member become so involved in wanting to hurt those who had hurt her that she became so bitter and ornery no one liked her or wanted to be with her. She died a lonely, sad person and never understood what her hatred had done to her. She would not be talked out of that feeling but rather fed on it with a vengeance that controlled her. I tried, as did others, to help her see this anger was destroying her but she would only say she wouldn't give the people who had hurt her satisfaction in knowing she had forgiven them. I don't think she knew she suffered much more than they did. They went on with their lives, maybe not even aware of what they had done. She carried her pain for so many years I often wondered if she wasn't afraid to let it go as she wouldn't know what to put in its place in her life. It seemed to energize her.

The rage we feel when deeply hurt by someone can cause us to strike out and physically harm them which happens too often. It doesn't take a lot of deep hurt to cause this reaction. Too many carry such pain and grief caused by others that they react immediately to the least perceived slight or remark that puts them back into that painful place.

Our entertainment media seems to nurture this reaction much too well and in the process demeans the real problems by even laughing at them, thinking that it is right to avenge the hurt. I guess if we make light of it things will get better. Wrong. Deep rooted pain and sorrow can only be made better by digging it out of our hearts and minds and getting rid of it. Some counseling helps but I found the best way was to turn them all over to the Lord, one at a time, until I could see them in the real light of what happened, maybe understand what caused them and become able to forgive. I didn't say forget!

At times I came to realize that my anger and maybe hate stemmed from anger at God because he had not helped me or protected me when I needed to be protected. That is hard to admit here, it was even harder to admit to myself. I know I have tried His patience many times when I felt He didn't do something the way I thought it should have been done. Read some of the other chapters and you will see how mouthy I have gotten with Him. Amazingly, I have learned that He might have a better idea than I do of what needs to be done.

You have your own knowledge of hate so you can come up with your own definition.

## CHAPTER 17

# *Anger*

FIRST LET ME TELL you that growing up in a family that thought it was something to be proud of to have a temper and use it handily had programmed me to develop a temper of my own. I learned to control it most of the time but could only be pushed so far before striking back at whatever or whoever was irritating me. I developed my rule of three, a person could hurt me twice and I would let it pass. The third time I would try to verbally destroy them.

A few years ago at a Lenten study group we were talking about the time to come when the lion will lay down with the lamb, a parable about what true peace will be like. The lion of course is the warrior and the lamb would be the victim. When I commented that I still, at my age, had to be careful not to let anything waken my sleeping lion, others laughed and didn't believe I had a lion in my personality. I guess it speaks well for my behavior and control over the past many years that they have not seen this side of me.

I'm not sure when anger that is stored up and carried

for a long time becomes hate or hatred if the anger is bad enough. I can only speak of what happened to me when an incident occurred that caused the lid on my box of pain to fly off and all hell to break loose. My lion woke up and took charge. I would do what had to be done. After the abuses of my childhood, the ugly shootings and killing, and a fatal illness that was destroying my body had filled that box so full there was no storage room left, the final blow came when a young woman in my family was assaulted. I won't go into details here to protect her privacy. A continuing harassment of the family by phone calls and someone knocking on their door caused tension and distress for her and all of us.

The total loss of control led me one night to take a shotgun and track a person through the snow in a blizzard with every intention of killing the guy who made those tracks. I have hesitated a long time in writing this as I still have a problem dealing with the idea I could consider such a thing. I share it now because you need to know what storing up the bad things in your life without coming to grips with them can do to you. It can cause you to become part of what I called at the time the lunatic fringe. That is what happened to me. I was enraged at the act itself, that the police were inept at best and just downright useless at worst. Superwoman once again came forth and would protect her family. The illness that was destroying me be damned, I was out to avenge this wrong and every wrong done to me in my life.

My reasoning was that if I shot someone I could get off easier with the law than your dad. People would just think I was crazy which was close to being the case by then. Judges would take a kinder view of a woman doing this than a man, especially one who had been an officer of the law at one time. I don't know if that would be true but that was the way I thought and even Dad could not stop me. Maybe he knew I would not be able to shoot someone as I had no idea how to use a shotgun. I don't think he was too worried as he probably had unloaded the gun before we got to the car and knew I wasn't dangerous to anyone but myself. He would let me work my anger out in this way. However it happened, my intent was there to destroy the person who harmed one of my family.

When someone kept harassing my family in their home I took this action. This had been brewing for a few days. When I couldn't sleep at times I would think up horrible things I would do to this guy if I could catch him. As all this broke loose into action I was very calm and methodical as I followed footprints in the snow. Dad drove the car beside me with headlights showing the way. The street by my family's house went up a steep hill and as I got to the top of the hill I lost all body heat as I wasn't wearing a coat or gloves, just a thin shirt and slacks and snow boots. I also had worn out all the anger on that steep climb and had to stop to catch my breath. As I stood there I heard, aloud or in my mind, the Lord ask me, you foolish child, can you really kill someone. Those words brought me to my senses, I got in the car and we went home after telling our family things were okay.

I sit here in disbelief as I write this. From this I learned to deal with serious things immediately rather than storing them as I had in all those years of my life. I cite again a line from a gospel song, "pull back the curtain Lord, show me where you brought me from and where I might have been." I know the Lord took over for me that night and saved me from making a horrible mistake.

## CHAPTER 18

# Forgiveness and How to Use It

FORGIVING IS NOT EASY. It sometimes takes months or even years if the damage done is so bad and hurtful you can't seem to overcome it. It isn't covered by simply saying, that's okay, I'll get over it. How about, it doesn't really matter that much or I just won't think about it and it will go away, I don't want to lose my relationship with him or her. I'm stronger than that so I can handle it, don't give it another thought. Or maybe like Scarlett O'Hara said, I'll think about that tomorrow. But tomorrow never comes to think about it.

Those reactions will keep you from facing the hurt you feel but they will also start the journey of hiding them in your mind and heart until you think you have forgotten about them. Don't kid yourself. Until you can search your heart and mind and maybe even understand what and why this happened, you are carrying that pain inside. Without realizing it, this has an effect and colors every day of your life. You see through a distorted lens. When you come to understand what the stuffed anger and hurt is doing to you, then you will be able to deal with it and honestly say, I forgive that person. Only then will you be free of the resentment and anger you have carried all this time. I can assure you from my own experience this is the most freeing, wonderful feeling you can imagine. You no longer have to carry this pain. I don't know who first said to forgive is to free a prisoner from his chains and discover I am that prisoner.

One thing I have learned is the person who hurt you may have gone on with life without another thought for you, while you carried this pain within you. Sometimes they do not know they have wounded you and would not have deliberately done so. Whether they did it intentionally or not is their problem. Their actions are theirs to deal with and if we are judged some day, their actions for them to answer for.

Don't think that forgiving means you are weak or fearful. It takes a strong person to look with honest eyes into his heart and mind and be able to say, I forgive. Jesus gave us the model for this as he was hanging on the cross. "Forgive them Father for they not what they do."

Forgiving doesn't mean you want to become bosom buddies with the one you are forgiving. If they are important enough in your life to go back and be friends, do so. Forgiving doesn't mean forgetting either. No where in the Bible does it say forgive and forget. It just says we have to forgive, seven times seventy if necessary. By forgiving it will become easier so you don't think about the hurt and it will gradually sink into a distant memory that doesn't walk with you every day.

An example of this: a young boy walked up to a tiger which immediately bit the boy's arm. The boy ran away, and then knowing this was the tiger's nature, the boy forgave the tiger. But the boy did not go back to the tiger again.

If you want the person who hurt you back in your life, go for it. But be aware you might be hurt again.

To forgive is an act of love toward people who have hurt us in some way but it is also an act of love toward ourselves. We are lovable people and don't need to be defined by someone else's words or deeds. We and the Lord make that determination, not others.

I have found that the hardest forgiveness to accomplish is forgiveness of my self. Many others have told me this is true for them too. When we continue to ask God to forgive us for something over and over, it means we haven't accepted His forgiveness. We kid ourselves into thinking our sin is so bad God couldn't possibly forgive us. This is gross pride on our part. In effect it says my sin is greater than God's love for me, when Jesus died on the cross that wasn't enough to overcome my sin. To say His life wasn't enough to overcome our wrong doings is denying the gift so freely given by Him. Remember though, He also said, go and sin no more.

The first thing we need to do is recognize our sin and then ask God's forgiveness. He already knows about it but wants us to acknowledge it in ourselves so we can get our act together and stop doing what is hurting us so badly. So don't be afraid to talk to Him and ask for forgiveness. It may be easier to start with a small sin than tackling the big ones! Practice makes it easier to step up and admit we are all sinners in some way. There was only one perfect man and He was crucified on the Cross. He lived as a human and understands what our lives are like, the temptations, the meanness and actions of others toward us and ours against others. God is all knowing so I don't think our finite minds can think of any new way to shock Him. Perhaps that is what we think we are doing when we say our sin is too great for God to forgive.

A short time after my episode of the journey through a blizzard with a shotgun happened I decided I'd had enough of trying to run my life since I was making a mess of it. I also knew that only the intervention of the Lord on that hilltop stopped me from doing something really terrible. We had started going back to church by now with a new priest, Father Chap Cranmer, who over time helped me work through a lot of bad memories. I felt I needed a one-on-one visit with God in a place of peace and quiet so I went to the church, only one there, and knelt to pray.

As I knelt there in total silence I told Jesus I was giving over all control of my life and asked if He would please help me make order out of the mess I had made of it. A different voice this time! A cold, vicious voice said, you fool what if there is no God. I was being whispered by the voice of evil. As stunned as I was, I knew this was the voice of real evil and could only think of what Jesus had said when tempted, "get thee behind me Satan". When I said those same five words, all the weight I had carried all those years fell away and I felt like I had been washed clean of every bad, ugly thing I had ever been through. After a few weeks of continuing to pray for my family and myself, I finally could honestly and intentionally pray for the soul of the one who attacked my family member. That was a real eye opener when I could do that.

Since that time many years ago I have tried to keep my side of the agreement and be and do what He asks of me. I fail at times. I spend time saying "sorry, forgive me" far too many times for me to feel sure of myself or comfortable enough not to keep in touch with Him all the time. He knows I keep trying.

A special ceremony called healing of memories is so helpful when we struggle with things we have carried for so long we don't know we still have them with us. This should be done with someone trained in the way of doing this to be most effective. You can do it yourself after learning how it is done. It is a simple act of reliving the incident that is so painful, only this time seeing it with Jesus holding your hand and walking with you. After dealing with the pain, heartache and sorrow that comes with doing this, we can with the Lord's help, forgive either the one who hurt us or forgive ourselves. I would suggest you have someone go through this with you rather than doing it alone. Most clergy are more than willing to help with this as are Christian counselors. I say Christian here because it does involve Jesus and non-Christians might not include Him in their treatment.

A subject of much discussion is Judas' betrayal of Jesus to the Pharisees that resulted in Jesus' crucifixion. Some think Judas had the idea that Jesus had come to overthrow the Roman rulers and drive them from his country, to restore the Jewish people to their rightful place in the land. When he found out that this was not what Jesus meant to do, that His kingdom was not of this world, he took it upon himself to try to force Jesus to do what he wanted. No one can know what Judas really thought. He was the money keeper for the group of apostles and some think he was caught stealing and acted out of revenge against his accusers and their leader, Jesus.

Whatever the reasoning behind his betrayal, he acted on it. Did it have to happen this way as some thing for our salvation to be assured. No one knows this side of the veil separating us from heaven. Did Jesus forgive Judas.

I recently watched a short documentary of World II. I lived through this time so I know some of the horrors that were happening. We didn't have all the means of communications that we have today so we only got glimpses through the news reels shown at the movies or the news on our radio. It was enough to let us know what a dangerous time we were living in. As I watched this documentary pictures of the maniacal behavior of Hitler I wondered, *was he forgiven for the millions who died by his orders*. Perhaps! If he confessed his sins and repented did he have to beg for forgiveness. Are there limits on how many sins and how big they are before they would not be forgiven. Do my sins seem small compared to those of Judas and Hitler. I don't want to be too sure Jesus uses a measurement which makes that comparison.

Nelson Mandela is a recipient of the Nobel Peace Prize. He was born in a small village in South Africa where his father was the village chief. As a young man he became aware of the unfairness of the rule of apartheid. The white people who had immigrated to that country became the elite ruling class. You can look up his story for more information on the effect this had on the native peoples.

At one time during the protests against apartheid Mr. Mandela was arrested and sentenced to life in prison where he suffered a great deal. He was a prisoner for twenty seven years until apartheid was finally overthrown. When freed he spoke most of forgiveness of those who had abused him so badly. He said to not forgive is like drinking a glass of poison and waiting for our enemy to die. This speaks so clearly of how hate and being unforgiving poisons our lives, our thoughts and causes us great harm. .

I have a newspaper clipping that has turned yellow with age. It gives no credit for who said it but it is profound: Give some thought to this bit of philosophy expressed by a Hebrew scholar, if we could read the secret history of those we would like to punish, we would find in each life enough grief and suffering to make us stop wishing anything more on them.

# Chapter 19

# Sin-The Result of Emotions

DEFINITION: IMMORAL ACT THOUGHT to be against divine law.

So now we come to the biggie, sin. Have you been waiting to see what I do with this one. You notice it is last in this section and that's because all of the mentioned emotions can cause us to sin. Therefore I left it for last. Since I am the writer I can do what I want with it.

I don't mean to make light of it at all and believe me I have sinned enough to fill two or three more chapters if I cared to share them. But I don't want to bore you. You have your own to think about .

Sin, people prefer not even say the word let alone define it or decide if it has anything to do with them. The rigorous, righteous, judgmental people think they have it pinned down and maybe they do. In some folks' book it only applies to acts that are whispered about behind a hand close to your ear, all the while gloating in the telling. Sorry if this offends some but what I have been taught and found to be true is sin doesn't only deal with immoral behavior but the many things we do every day. The word immoral is used in many ways but usually deals with sexual misdeeds or murder or, or, or, on and on. There are also sins of omission not just commission, those being the things we should have done but didn't do. When we don't help someone in need, someone ill or needing help in any way, that is sin of omission. If you aren't familiar with the parable of the Good Samaritan read it in the gospel of Luke 10: 25 through37.

I have come to believe that sin is anything that stands between God and me. That is a huge area to be caught up in. I tell you that we are not humans having a spiritual experience, we are spiritual beings having a human experience. I truly believe in the Holy Trinity. We are God's people whom He loved enough that His Son died for the salvation of our souls. In his book, *Glimpses of the Devil* Scott Peck says, the place of the soul is so deep that it is the most private part of a human, the most private of our private parts, a place where only God can enter. In case you can't grasp that, it does not refer in any way to our reproductive parts or any other physical part of us. Just thought I should clear that up.

So back to sin being anything that stands between God and me. There is a whole list in the Bible that isn't covered in the Ten Commandments, implied but not named in the Commandments. The ones that come to mind are envy, pride, greed, sloth, anger, vengeance, apathy, jealousy, gluttony, drunkenness, selfish ambition, arrogance, malice, heresy, conceit, placing oneself as equal to God, and there are several more I'm sure. As you read this list you can tell the harm each one does to you or another person.

The one told of in the Bible as being the unforgiven sin is the sin against the Holy Spirit. To blaspheme against or deny the Spirit is the one sin God won't overlook or forgive. I am not sure what this means but I think it is because the Holy Spirit is sent from God and Jesus and is a part of them, so to deny the Holy Spirit is to deny them too. I am open to hear other's thoughts on this.

Most sins are told in parables or other parts of the Bible. They can occupy our minds to the extent that we don't have time to enjoy and celebrate what we do have. These can and do make us forget that we are God's people and get in the way of becoming friendly with Him. I know hearing this will surprise some of you, to think we can be friends with God. He is waiting for us to let it happen. We have to make the first step toward friendship with Him as He won't push into our lives without our inviting Him in.

# Chapter 20

## Emotions Come From Within Us

When we become so wrapped up in ourselves that only our way is right, only our way will make us happy, only our minds can have all the answers, that my dears is sin. It shuts God out of our lives. That is not a healthy place to be. I have been there and know of what I speak. I was supermom when I became so angry with God that I thought I could do nicely without Him or His advice. Big pride! It is a mighty big fall from that high peak of thinking we don't need him, a bigger fall when our pride dumps us flat on our face. In my case it was a painful and pain filled time of slowly working my way back to the truth of what reality is in this world.

Reality is not the false faces everyone puts on to impress others. It isn't the false images the entertainment world hands out. Remember folks doing the entertaining, be it sports or media people, finish their days work and go home to their own real world. It might not be the same type of world you live in but it is not the imaginary world they make their living in. Some still try to live in that false world but you can read about how destructive that is for them. They too have troubles and sadness. Do not be envious of them. No one gets out of this world without some heartache and sorrow, even the rich, the warriors and those who control our lives.

No one seems to get by in life without being harmed in some way, sometimes by people who think they do us a favor but are misguided. Others knowingly take advantage of a friendship. One of your dad's good friends did this to him when selling us a gas station. The term used in those days was blue sky, selling something that didn't exist. The amount of blue sky involved in the buying of the business was so great that when the time came that we had to sell it, the difference between the buying and selling price put us in debt for three years. After struggling for two years to make a living the decision was made to sell the business. We found out that every little scrap of metal, old pieces of tires that should have been discarded and more junk was included on the inventory when we bought the business. Dad had not gone through every item at the time of purchase, trusting his friend to be honest. As a result I had to go to work to help us get by and pay off that debt. That was a gift to me as the job was one I enjoyed greatly for many years.

As I watched your dad suffer the pain of betrayal by a good friend there wasn't much forgiveness in my heart for a long time. He was devastated that a friend would do this to him. Adding to the hurt, this good friend never bought a gallon of gas from us. Nothing could be said or done to ease the anguish Dad felt. Later he was more forgiving than I could be. The friendship of course stopped. Like the boy and the tiger I mentioned earlier, Dad didn't go back to be bitten again. When he was asked to be a pallbearer at this old friend's funeral Dad said yes and did it with no hard feelings. I, in my hurt of watching Dad go through such pain, thought it was rather fitting that this came to be. When I said something to him about the circle coming full, he had forgotten about the cost of the friendship and had forgiven his lost friend. My work on forgiving took longer than it should have but I was still angry with God and saw only another cheap hurt. I think it is worse to watch a loved one suffer hurts than to go through them your self.

I haven't told many things about your dad's life as that would was his story to tell and I don't know what that might be. I do know that his growing up years were very painful at times and yet full of love and good times too.

He told me about a time that had to do with his mother, your grandma Dorothy, when she was the postmaster of the small coal mining camp where they lived. The post office was in the company store so she also was hired to be a clerk there. These were the days during World War II and a lot of food items were restricted by government controls that gave most fresh food to the armed forces.

Fruits were only available when in season and weren't available year round as they are today. Bananas were a great luxury. When a shipment came in they were allotted to families according to the number of people in the family.

Dad and your grandmother got what was allotted for two and that was all. Some of the boys in the camp would tease your dad and make snide remarks about Grandma Dorothy because he had bananas in his school lunch for more days than they did. They didn't know that your grandma didn't eat her bananas but saved hers for Dad so he could have the nutrition he needed. There were many other instances of hurts he suffered in those days and I think he came to understand that those people were acting out of their own anxieties or pain. He chose to forgive them for a lot but someone had done something to him that was so bad he wouldn't or couldn't share it with me. As we talked about all the hurts in our lives one day he hinted about this but I asked him about it he said it was too awful to tell me. I don't know if he ever told anyone but he never got past it until the day he died.

Lessons are repeated until they are learned. A lesson will be presented to you in various forms until you have learned it. When you have learned it you can go on to the next lesson. If you are alive, that means there are still lessons to be learned.

As old as I am, I still learn something all the time. My outlook has changed about so many things. I have learned over time that the only people who can hurt me are those who matter to me, my family and friends. Most others are simply people who happen to be in my life for a time. If they do something that causes me problems or pain they also have added something good to my life in some way. I have learned something from them. Everyone in my life has been necessary to help me be who I have become.

I promised I wouldn't preach so will stop here. I hope I have given you enough ideas about these topics and how they affect your relationship with the Lord that you will search on your own for the foundation you want to build with Him.

# CHAPTER 21

## Virtue and Honesty

GOOD AND USEFUL QUALITIES. A virtuous person is good, kind, helpful, moral and good to know. An honest person does not cheat, lie or steal.

Honesty is a virtue. This is a tough one to describe well. The opposite of honesty of course is a lie. When is it okay to tell a lie. We all have our own opinions on that. If a lie will cause some one trouble or hurts them in any way it should not be told. Degrees of lies cause confusion for most. There are white lies, fibs and the big bad ones. Today the use of lies seem to be more acceptable than in past years, no matter the reason.

A co-worker at the drugstore where I worked as a teenager passed an ugly remark about a young woman walking by the store. Not only was it gossip but it was a lie. The young woman was going with a fellow who she soon married. And the kicker is that I found out later the woman passing the remark had done the same thing she had said about the woman she gossiped about. The gossiper had been sleeping around with several guys when she was single. This goes back to the subject of the untamable tongue.

Isn't this a fun subject.

I treasured being honest and had been taught while growing up that to lie was bad. Most of us were taught as we grew up that if you couldn't say something good about someone don't say anything at all. Your grandma Lou quoted someone by saying she would rather deal with a thief than a liar. A thief can only take your material things. A liar can steal your good name, or harm you in so many ways. A liar cannot be trusted to tell the truth no matter the occasion. I have a built-in reaction to liars. When a person lies to me I will never again believe anything they say. If the lie is something that comes against me I will accost that person and make sure they correct the lie they have told to those to whom they said it. I do this nicely but firmly. Not many have made the mistake of lying about me more than once. A few members of my family have found this to be true too. Although I still love them, I let them know that lying to me or about me is not a good thing to do.

To this day if someone would say I had told a lie I would go to that person and get to the heart of the matter as to why it was said. I know from experience how much harm can be done by lies. The idea of mean girls isn't anything new. It was alive and well when I was growing up. Those mean, lying girls were left alone by the rest of us after we learned our lesson of being hurt by their meanness.

I worked at several places as I became old enough. I was a clerk and soda jerk at one of the drugstores. Bet you don't know what that term means. We had a fountain where soft drinks were made by us along with malts, sundaes and other good stuff. Soft drinks didn't come only in a bottle in those days. The drinks were called sodas and we had to pump a handle on different flavored syrups to get the syrup in the glass before adding carbonated water to make the soda. Thus the name soda jerk. Nothing derogatory about it.

We also waited on customers for other merchandise. At one time I could name almost every fishing fly available. We had to be able to find the one a customer wanted in a stack of maybe twenty or more boxes. Not just any fly would do, it had to be the one the customer wanted and he knew what it looked like.

At the end of the fountain for cokes and malts was a humidor that held cigars. I still wonder what the difference is in cigars to cause so many kinds being made. They all smell bad to me and I would never smoke one so I don't know the difference. When a customer wanted to buy a cigar he would point to or name the one he wanted and we would take out the box of cigars and let him pick out his own. We were never allowed to touch them as we might crush or bruise one! I don't know if it is still done in that manner.

One day a young girl about ten years old came in with a list of items her grandmother had sent to be filled. I got all the things on the list, sacked them, took her money and handed her the change. In those days we could make change by doing the math in our head without using a machine of any kind. If a people couldn't do that they didn't work in a job handling money.

A short time later my boss called me to his office and told me the girl's grandmother called and told him I had kept the change instead of giving it to the girl. The girl, on seeing the money, had bought herself some candy that she apparently ate before reaching home. I was furious that I was accused of stealing. I explained to my boss and he said he would take care of it. I asked if I could take care of it and he said that would be okay. When my shift ended I marched to that person's house and in very firm words told her just what had happened. She called her granddaughter to the door, questioned her and found out the truth. The woman apologized but I never felt comfortable around her again and certainly didn't trust the girl.

I guess I believe that honesty is the best policy with a white lie allowed to spare someone's feelings regarding an ugly dress. See how easy it is to make room for our own behavior. When my good friend and I stopped at the local dress store, our boss was there trying on dresses. She had on a dress we thought didn't look good on her. She asked our opinions, my friend just turned and walked away without saying a word. I told her I thought it looked nice on her. I said this to spare her feelings because it was a pretty dress but it wasn't right for her according to my way of seeing it. But it pleased her to hear it and she may have bought the dress. How wrong is it to spare someone's feelings in what we feel is a minor thing.

In this day and social morass of ideas about what is right and wrong it is hard to tell you how to know the truth or a lie. You already know what is right and what isn't.

It is right to be honest with others and especially with

yourselves. You might get by with a little fib here and there to yourself but you won't fool God so don't even try.

He knows you better than you know yourself and you can hide nothing from Him. I recommend Psalm 139 to tell you that no matter where you go, to the sky or the sea or to the grave He knows where and who you are. Makes you think, huh. It isn't meant to be scary or threatening but rather comforting that you are important enough to Him that He is watching out for you. Be honest and honor yourself without taking the credit away from God. To Him goes the glory for whatever right we are strong enough to do. Just though I'd throw that tidbit in as I'm not sure where else to put it! I am an amateur writer after all.

# CHAPTER 22

# *Your Eyes and Mine*

MATTHEW IN CHAPTER 6 talks about our eyes being a lamp of our soul. I have heard it said the eyes are the window of the soul. Matthew goes on to explain that if your eyes are bad your entire being is bad. Perhaps that means that with "bad" eyes you can only see that which is bad in the world and cannot see the good or beauty. It speaks more to who you are in your innermost part. In Scott Peck's book *Glimpses of the Devil,* the place of the soul is so deep that it is the most private part of a human, the most private of our private parts, a place only God may enter. I know, I know, I have I have quoted this before but it is too good not use it again.

If you follow ideas about how you can read eyes you will be told that when someone is speaking to you if they look down and to their left they are being less than truthful. Really! When I am talking to people on serious matters my eyes roam from left to right, across the room as I try to get my thoughts together before I say any thing. It is hard for me to think deeply while looking right into someone's eyes and trying to tell them my thoughts at the same time.

However I have found that when you look into people's eyes you can sometimes see the pain they are in, the sorrow they carry or the happiness they are enjoying. Other eyes have shown me a peace beyond my understanding, being aware of what the people are dealing with.

A woman who had a large family and whose husband was permanently disabled and couldn't work to support them had the kindest eyes ever. When she looked at me her eyes shone with an inner peace and love that was wonderful to see. I had known her for some time but I remember the day I waited on her as a customer at the drugstore and was unable to understand how she could be in such a peaceful place. A grandchild of two or three years of age had drowned just a few weeks earlier. In thinking about her later I knew the Lord was holding her close to Him with comfort and peace. That peace was reflected through her eyes. I will never forget her face as she smiled so gently at me.

I have seen many people whose eyes are like this. They are blessed with peace and love and it shines through. Others have nice eyes that smile and I know they are happy but not all have the special glow of the peace of the Lord.

Others who have had great sorrow and bad times have turned hard and mean natured. Perhaps they didn't know the love of Jesus and didn't find His comfort for them. Their eyes show their feelings into the world.

Of course if the eyes are the windows into the soul the bad shows up too. I have seen several people who I mistrusted and was proven right because their eyes showed me their cause was not good. Their actions were harmful in many ways.

One was a reformed gangster who had become a traveling preacher. He was a huge, tall and obese man. His eyes were blue but hard, almost as cold as the diamond rings he wore. He had two companions who were big muscular men. The preacher was being advertised as to his repenting being true. All wore suits, as young as I was I could see quality in their suits. The preacher had come to town in answer to an invitation from a local small church. He may have been reformed but had not given away the spoils of his previous life style. He wore rings with the biggest diamonds I have ever seen and his two companions always walked one on each side of him like body guards. Two of my friends and I met them on the street one day and got a close look at those rings. The three men walked by us without even seeing us. We girls decided he should have gotten rid of the spoils of his previous life if he was serious about being converted. We thought he was hiding out from someone by traveling through small towns. Perhaps we were completely off the mark but we were of the opinion that reforming and repenting should have included giving up all the finery he had gained in his earlier life. Now that was being judgmental on our part I know, but we also were making a judgment on what repenting should mean as a lesson for ourselves.

One evening a group of us were walking by the vacant store where the revival was taking place. We stood quietly just outside the open door to listen. Two of the girls shoved me into the room and my momentum carried me a few feet down the aisle. The reformed preacher looked at me and asked if I needed his help. I said no, thanked him and left. My friends had gone on up the street and were laughing like fools. I gave them a good idea of how embarrassed and mad I was but they couldn't stop laughing. I finally had to agree with them that it was kind of funny.

Another time I had an opportunity to work with a man who was supposed to be helping a situation in Kremmling. He was from Denver and was CEO of a large corporation. His eyes were totally black with no light shining from them. The only way I could describe them was that there was nothing behind them, as if nothing was good and I didn't trust him. Lack of trust turned out to be right as we found out later. He had been hired to help us out in a public institution and instead was trying to close us down so our business would go to the corporation he worked for. We didn't let him stay long. He went back to Denver without his mission being accomplished.

A few who live their life wholly for the Lord and His work have eyes you can almost see through. A favorite bishop had eyes that made me think that looking into the Lord's eyes must be like that. A woman who prayed with people for healing, had blue eyes that were so clear and bright I felt I was able to see the Lord in them.

I am sorry to say I have seen little children who at one time had bright shiny eyes and then had dull, sad eyes that spoke of some kind of abuse or pain they couldn't deal with and couldn't find a way to get help. I have had eyes that stormed anger and pain at me as I could not keep a promise of safety I had made to a boy who was being badly abused.

The situation was taken out of my hands by the police, his parents were into heavy drug use and selling. I still wonder how that boy turned out. I know he was later removed from his home by the law but I haven't heard about him since. He would be in his thirties now. I just pray he is okay and enjoying life, that what was happening to him didn't totally defeat him.

When I worked at the school, students would share their problems with me. My sons were almost their age so I guess they felt I was an adult they could trust. The counselor at that time was not liked by the students and they wouldn't go to him which made him dislike me. He thought I was taking his job but I couldn't help what the students felt about him. If they wanted to talk to me I wasn't going to turn them away. They would start talking and their eyes would be sad and their faces drawn and angry. As they talked through their problems and found answers their eyes would be bright and shiny again. Even today some of the girls stay in touch.

Eyes that really shine with joy can be seen in newly weds and their families, new parents of babies, and of course grandparents who are absolutely giddy with joy. Look at the faces and joy filled eyes of people who have just been baptized into the family of Jesus. That is a joy for all to share.

## CHAPTER 23

# Eyes Speak of Good or Bad

SEVERAL OF THE CHURCHES in Grand County had organized a group called the Good Samaritans, taken from the Bible story of the Good Samaritan. You can find this in the gospel of Luke 10: 30 through 36. I mentioned it an earlier chapter so I repeat it as a good lesson. An agreement was made with restaurants, hotels and motels, grocery stores and gas stations to accept the vouchers we handed out to people in need, those traveling through the country as well as the local folks. I was one of those who had the vouchers to hand out for whatever services were necessary.

One of the times I remember looking into a person's eyes that stays with me happened when a local policeman called about two fellows needing a room and some food. The police always checked the travelers for us so we would be safe. I met them at a local hotel where the necessary papers for supper, breakfast and room for the night were filled out. Those fellows' story was quite sad. They were in the country illegally, having come in to work in the harvests in eastern Colorado and then left to their own devices to survive. This was about twenty five years ago so no fuss about the illegal thing was made. They had hopped a freight train in Denver, thinking it would take them south but the train brought them west into the mountains. They were discovered and booted off in Bond, Colorado. They managed to get on another freight train headed east. They were found out and made to detrain in east Grand County. One of the members of the Samaritan group found them and brought them to Kremmling to the police and thus I became involved.

I needed a signature on the vouchers for a room and meals before I could release them and only one of the men could write his name. As he signed I watched and saw him sign Jesus and his last name which I don't remember. The first name startled me and when he finished signing he looked at me. I found myself looking into the deepest, kindest eyes I have ever seen. I thought, *I am looking into the eyes of Jesus.* When I could breathe again we just went on with the transaction and I walked away.

In Hebrews 13:2 we are told to be kind to strangers as they might be angels and we won't be aware that they are until it might be too late. Old Testament lessons tell of God's messengers, angels, visiting different people. We don't know or understand what the Lord is doing at any given moment so we are never wrong to reach out and help someone in need. Maybe they were angels. I can't say aye or nay, just telling you what I saw in the man's eyes. They were two of God's people anyway.

The police told me they would see the fellows were headed in the right direction to get home, by bus or train so I no longer had any connection with them but hoped they made it to their home, wherever that might be.

So look closely at people you meet. You never know who you may be talking to. I am not suggesting you accost people just to look into their eyes without a reason. They might think you are up to no good!

Another time your dad and I were asked to let a woman who was traveling through the country stay at our house until the bus came through on its way west. The man who headed up the Samaritan group called us. He lived in the east end of the county and would find these wanderers along the road and help them find transportation. We said sure, she could stay with us for that time. By the time she was brought to our house at about one p.m. we had found out the bus didn't come through town until midnight.

We didn't want to stay up that late trying to keep a stranger entertained and fed. We decided since it was such a nice day and we didn't have anything else to do we would take her to Craig, Colorado where people would be waiting to help her along her journey, instead of waiting for the bus. The group leader had arranged for a church in Craig to house her for the night and then put her on a bus to her destination. He had bought a bus ticket for her from Kremmling to Craig which could be redeemed when we took her to Craig by car. We were a bit surprised when she refused to shake our hands when we welcomed her but didn't press the point. We were more surprised when she refused to let this fellow help her take her belongings out of his car. She told him in less than a kind way, "I've had all the help I ever want from you" and took care of her things herself. By now we weren't sure just how to proceed with this plan. Her tone of voice warned us to not offer help either. We found out later she was finding rides to get to Montana and how she managed I don't know. As we watched her load her things into our large car, her belongings filled the trunk and most of the back seat. She had a lot of possessions.

She sat behind me in the car and wouldn't talk until we were a few hours on the road. I have to say I was a little nervous thinking *if she is a deranged person or a robber and she is sitting right behind me.* Then finally she told us her first name, Gloria, and shared a little of her story. She was trying to get home to her family.

As I write this part about eyes I can recall the look she gave that fellow when she refused his help. She glared at him. It was a jolt when we got to Craig and found he had made no arrangements for her with anyone, church or otherwise. The pastor at the church was surprised as he knew nothing of this sort being done. We also found out later that there may not have been a bus ticket for her to anywhere. She didn't have it with her and we had not seen one. Our only recourse was to take her to the police where they knew how to get food and a bed for and put her on the road the next day, not a bus! When I asked why it was done in this way, they said that was the practice, just put people like her on the road at the edge of town and let them go. She thanked us for being kind to her and trying to help. We didn't have any spare money to buy a bus ticket for her so all we could do was pray with for her safe arrival at her home.

Some time later we found out why she was so angry with that man when he was exposed as to his actions. He was found to be gathering these homeless women and using them for his pleasure for a while and then dumping them on someone else to take care of. I then fully understood the look in her eyes toward him and the snarl in her voice. Instead of being the ungrateful person I thought her to be, I knew if she had said something about it to us we would have taken care of him immediately, notifying the police to arrest him. She didn't trust anyone though so didn't tell us about it. Her eyes were wounded as was her very soul.

He was an ordained pastor but didn't have a church. As I write this I am shaking my head in disgust and amazement that a man supposedly trained to serve the Lord would behave in such a way. It also made us realize he had deliberately lied to us as to the arrangements made for her. How many others he had hooked into this behavior we will never know but I don't think we were the first ones he lied to. I know it happens all the time but I still can't understand how people can do this. Later he was found out as to his behavior but I don't know if he was prosecuted. I don't suppose there was anyone around to press charges as all his victims had been moved out of the area by then, using people like us to do his moving them.

## Chapter 24

# What I See With My Eyes

As I have worked on the chapter about people's eyes I stopped for a while to think about what I see, aside from eyes. Rather what do I see when I just look out of my eyes. This is what came to mind. I see the world around me, the blue sky or white, depending on the weather, the green grass and leaves on trees. I think how amazing it is that my ancestors forever back have looked at the same blue sky, not the same green grass or trees but surely something green from their time. Because God created it to be looked at and enjoyed it goes on from one generation to another. From creation to forever until that time when God will proclaim, "It is finished!" and Jesus comes to claim His world.

Perhaps we are a work in progress. How did my ancestors see the sky and the green things of nature. Have we, I, grown more insightful as to God's hand in all things. Are we growing towards the place where we no longer worry or are anxious or do we plod along the same rutted road, generation after generation, not seeing God's plan for us. Do I trust Him more or less than my ancestors would trust him. Do we ever know the full presence and reassurance of He who loves us most because we are so intellectually brilliant that we know better than He knows. We know we must do and go to keep the world running in some semblance of order. Why can't we conceive of a plan that only requires us to be God's people in a place He made for us and come to the life style that uses the gifts He has given to us to enjoy.

As I was editing this part of my story I looked out across the patio and saw the resident squirrel charging around in the mad, wild manner of squirrels. It reminded me of some years ago after I had back surgery. My niece Pat was staying with me to help me for a few weeks. She had walked out on the patio and looked around. She came in and told me I had corn growing in the bark layers next to the fence. We went out to measure the stalks, the biggest was about five feet tall and two others were a bit shorter. I decided I would leave them to see what came of their appearance in the bark. Squirrels, aside from being a nuisance, are entertaining and apparently smarter than I give them credit for being. The corn continued to grow and the larger stalk had ears of corn growing, two getting to the stage called being in tassel. That means there was corn silk on the ends of the ears. I was lucky enough to be watching when one squirrel came tearing across the lawn with an ear of corn about three inches long in his mouth. He ran up a tree and settled into a notch of a branch and started his meal. He carefully peeled off the corn husks and threw them to the ground where another squirrel immediately started eating them. Meanwhile when the ear was clean of husks the first squirrel started eating corn on the cob the same way people do. Holding it in two paws he turned it around and around until it was cleaned of all corn. Then he threw it down to his buddy on the ground which grabbed it up and ran off with it. I don't know what it means when animals start growing their own food! The squirrels bury extra food where they can get it later and one had planted some corn from the neighbor's bird feeder. Sorry to say I haven't grown any corn since then. I did manage to get a fuzzy picture of the squirrel in the tree eating the corn.

Squirrels are entertaining but they are expensive pests when they eat through telephone wires at the main box. My phone was so noisy I had to call the company to find what the problem might be. The first place the service man checked was the outside box. The wire to my house was almost eaten through. The telephone company replaced the wire and hired a man to bury it. Everything was going well until the guy burying the wire cut a hose to my lawn sprinkler system. A call to the company that takes care of that system brought a repairman who needed some water to do something. The guy who takes care of my yard in the summer had left a hose attached to the outside faucet causing a pipe to freeze back into my house basement. When we turned on the outside water system water flowed right nicely into a room downstairs. Luckily my daughter-in-law Lisa was there and yelled to turn off the water at the main pipe. Then I had to call a plumber to replace the broken pipe inside the house. Total cost of day was close to five hundred dollars. Needless to say I am not crazy about squirrels even when they are being cute. I put these squirrel stories here because I know they too are part of God's kingdom and have a purpose but I'm not sure what that might be. I also would like to ask Him why we have mosquitoes.

The great mystery of God's plan isn't ours to know. We can accept that He is in charge, hears our crying and praying, our laughing. He lets us into His presence by saying hello to Him and inviting Him to be in our lives. We can sit and listen for Him to speak to us in a way we can hear and let Him help us along our pathways. I can contribute good or bad to my life and others' lives, my choice. But do my actions really change the outcome of it all. Only the end of my story will tell me that but I try to make a difference when I can and wherever I might be. I hope my eyes reflect into the world the peace I have found by letting the Lord be in my life. May it be so with you.

## Chapter 25

# Being Responsible for Our Actions

**Did Adam and Eve Set Us Up**

I want to make it clear that we all have to take responsibility for our behavior. At some time we will have to accept that we have made a mistake, hurt someone deeply or physically, caused someone trouble they don't deserve or need. I will use the story of Adam and Eve to help lay the groundwork for this section.

Definition: myth, a story used to explain a truth held by people of spiritual thinking.

Some hold that the story of Adam and Eve is a myth. If so, it's used to explain to primitive people how the world came be. If today we tried to explain to those folks in terms of physics or interplanetary travel, they wouldn't have a clue what we were talking about. I am not sure I understand a lot of the new things myself. There is more to it than just to explain creation. The story continues to tell us how humans have messed up from the beginning. It also tells of the sly way we have of turning the blame of what we do onto others' shoulders. If you haven't read the story please do so now so you can know what I am talking about. Read Genesis chapters 1 through 4.

When God called to Adam in the garden and Adam said he was hiding because he was naked, God wanted to know who had told Adam he was naked. And so the story goes. Adam says its Eve's fault for giving him the fruit of the tree of knowledge wherein he became aware of good and evil. Thinking himself evil by being naked he hid from God. Then Eve tells her part of the story blaming the serpent that tempted her to eat of the forbidden fruit. Adam even slyly suggests that it is all God's fault because He gave him this woman. Maybe if God hadn't made him a mate this would not have happened. Well, that may be better than saying I messed up.

These days we call it passing the buck or whatever is the newest term for not owning up to what we have done of our own free will. It takes a lot of courage to say I'm sorry or I shouldn't have done that, or just being brave enough to acknowledge that we are less than perfect and we make mistakes. Perfection is the goal set before us today in so many ways. The messages of entertainment, diets, beauty, etc. want us to be gods, perfect in every way. Sadly the goal has nothing to do with being the people God would have us be.

The happiest, healthiest people are those who accept themselves as they are, not perfect but happy with who they are. Not everyone can be an Einstein or Stephen Hawking or Marilyn Monroe or whomever the latest model of perfection might be. Their fame is fleeting and brings little peace of mind until they discover who they really are and live with that. So we need to do the same. Accept we have less than a genius mind, or beautiful looks by the world's standard, or a huge house, or the biggest car. Any thing that makes us less than we are in our own eyes is so destructive. Appreciate yourself. If God is happy with me I should be happy with me. We are responsible for what we do and not for what others do to us. We let ourselves off the hook by blaming others for making us into who we are and what others have done to us that cause us to act as we do. Nonsense! If you are able to read this sentence you should be able to understand that you are now able to make decisions on your own. Hopefully you have learned to make wise decisions through good sense, good teaching and knowing what is right and wrong just by living. I know your raising formed your ides of what life is about but you don't have to live in that image if it isn't who you want to be. I don't buy into the idea that potty training, for instance, warps kid's minds. That was a popular idea going around at one time. I don't know if it still is being used to explain some behaviors. If done properly it doesn't need to be blamed for anything. If it was done with violence, spankings for instance, that changes it into a mind set experience. But if not done at all think what it would be like to live in a society where people were not toilet trained! Not a pleasant thought.

Be mindful of those who crave fame and fortune and come up with cockamamie ideas just to become known in the world. I look back at some of these ideas along the years that were extremely weird or downright outrageous and dangerous. We had offers to buy into new amusement parks that never developed, diamonds guaranteed to be first class which turned out to be commercial grade, a savings and loan company that had wonderful rates of interest and was co-owned by a famous person. We saved our money as we didn't have any to spare to invest. All those great plans failed.

Remember what we always tried to teach you boys regarding the written word. Just because something is in print doesn't make it true. In the 1960's or70's a reporter for one of the Denver newspapers wrote about a group of people who, being offended by cattle in the fields being naked, decided to gather funds to put diapers on cows. Living in cattle country, we were all amazed to read this. A week later the reporter printed a follow-up story explaining he had done this to show how gullible people could be. There was no such group, no such problem with naked cows. His biggest problem was finding a way to return the monies people had sent him to fund putting diapers on cows! My question is would you have sent money in to this supposed group to diaper cows. This is known as using discernment, to be able to see the lies, or the deceptions in what you read. We also have the benefit of the Internet, cell phones and their use to spread news and some big lies. I know people who believe if they see it on the Internet it has to be true. Big danger here. Anyone can put the most incredible lie on the Internet and some people will believe it! I have read of some incredible ideas on my computer that are too good to be true.

Sometimes credible, trustworthy people are caught up in what we call scams. Scammers tell us something is real and we, without fully checking into their story, buy what they are selling. In this day of overt, dirty politics we are hammered by such nonsense and have to discern between truth and outright character damaging lies. This is hard for the average person to do as we don't have access to all the information we need to make a wise decision. We need to try.

I want to tell you not to let others name you. By that I mean tagging you with a name such as stupid, dull, boring, nerd, or ugly which can help us become the name. Don't believe them, unless of course you are doing things that will hurt you or others such as criminal, druggie, abuser. In that case shape up and stop that behavior now. When we allow others to call us names that demean us we are unable to recognize our talents, our gifts we were given by God at birth (maybe at conception)

When I worked in the school I was the district bookkeeper and what is now called the executive assistant to the superintendent of schools. I did the payroll each month and I delivered the teachers' pay checks each month during class time to save them from making a trip to my office . I did this as quietly as possible to not disturb the classes. One particular day I was in the fifth and sixth grades building, climbing the stairs to the classrooms. I don't know if it is still done this way but at that time each pupil would stand in front of the class and read a part of a story. I was stunned when I heard the teacher loudly say to the class, listen now and see if stupid here can read for us. I had to wait a little time to go into that room as I was furious with that teacher. That young boy, standing in front of the class, had just been named, a name the other kids would call him, a name that may have convinced him he was stupid. When I got back to my office I told the superintendent what I had heard. He said he would take care of it. I don't know what he did but that teacher was assigned new duties the next year. She never was in a classroom again. I am sure she was watched closely after that. She was given a hard schedule and retired a few years later. I wonder how many children she damaged over the years by this type of behavior.

God has a plan for all of us and we need to discover what that is. Find your special talent, be it music, art, homemaker, parent, care giver, medical field, one in which you will be happy. Nudges from the Lord and our own interests usually let us know what we would really like to do. Others who put labels on us don't know who we are or don't have a clue as to what God has given us to work with. Listen to what your inner most desires are. Hopefully they are legal! Pay attention. This is probably the line of work or career you will be most happy in doing. Maybe you won't get rich doing it but you will be much happier than working for big pay and hating the job.

You are only responsible for your actions. Why would I have to pay when the fellow down the street runs into someone with his car. Why would I say yes when asked if I helped a robber across town miles away. These are extreme examples but I am trying to make this point. If the Lord is keeping score, only your actions are credited to your account with Him. Did you do something nice for someone and the score will be good. Did you mess up which might be a demerit on your score sheet.

# Chapter 26

## *Happiness and Joy*

I BEGAN MY STORY using a quote on the first two lines of chapter one about life being what happens between events. As you have read by now, the events were good and bad, sometimes soul damaging with the Lord saving that soul. Those were the events that I wanted to use to tell you the Lord really does exist and helped me through all of them, if not at the moment of happening, then at a later time of total healing.

I have been told many times that being happy comes from within. We determine the mood we are in at any given time. I also know that after events happen it is hard sometimes to get back to a happy outlook on life. But it can be done. I have had lots of practice. .

When I look back over these many years I see so much happiness and at times real joy. Joy that comes from being cleansed by the Lord from my guilt and sorrow. Joy that overwhelms me in a way the word happiness doesn't quite cover. Joy of truly knowing deep within my soul that God,

Jesus and the Holy Spirit are real and involved in my life because I chose to let them become part of me

Happiness has been a big part of my life, overriding all the bad things that came about. After having shut down my emotions so many years earlier in response to such hard things my mind couldn't handle, I wonder if I have ever experienced full emotions of any kind. I feel happy but as I possibly see colors differently than others do, my happy may not be full happiness. There is no way of knowing the answer. My family, past generations and present, have always been important to me and to make any of my family happy makes me happy. Only as an adult, having grown past the self-interest of young years, have I had the fun of doing and being with family for all kinds of celebrations.

Your dad and I were married on December 30, 1950. Our wedding day was wonderful, although the town was almost snow bound and temperatures were very cold. Love had to keep us warm. The church was on a hillside above town and the streets were ice covered. My dad, Papa Bill, started up the icy street, got half way up it and had to back down to the level main street. He got a good run at that hill the second time. He was already nervous about walking me down the aisle so this icy street didn't help him or me. Mom was in the back seat and silent, maybe too worried to say anything. We made it up the hill to the church. When I stepped out of the car I came close to falling on the ice. In those days brides dressed at home, the small churches didn't have enough room for them to dress there. My mother, who was a wonderful seamstress, made my gown out of ten yards of white slipper satin. It had a train of some length too. As I managed to grab onto the car door handle and catch myself I had a picture of me walking down the aisle with a big snow blotch on the back of my beautiful gown. However, I made it into the church with lots of help.

Almost fifty four years of marriage hold sacred moments of such deep joy and blessings they too stand out. I say almost fifty four years as Dad died one month and six days short of our fifty fourth anniversary. Friends had surprised us on our twenty fifth anniversary and we had a special celebration on our fortieth anniversary. Our health was so poor at that time we thought we wouldn't make it to celebrate a fiftieth. We did however and had a wonderful celebration of fifty years together.

The birth of both of you boys, although scaring me witless, was one of those joys. I didn't know anything about babies and was afraid I would do something wrong or hurt you! The births of all the grandchildren were so special we never stopped feeling the wonderful joy of being grandparents. What a blessing they are. Being a part of the lives of parents, siblings, nieces, nephews, cousins and of course good friends meant happy times. Celebrating holidays, birthdays or just a time to be together blessed us for many years. Pulling together when tragedy struck or illness brought death also had a special closeness that bordered on, if not happy, at least a close love of each other.

Holiday preparations were happy times for me. We knew the real meaning was centered in the Lord but sometimes that would get lost in the all the going and doing. For Christmas I made the grandkids their special Santa sacks holding little toys they opened on Christmas Eve to help them wait for Christmas morning to open packages. When we went on picnics and Dad would fish we were out in a world that was a clean fresh new day, bringing a renewing touch to the hard work of that time in our lives.

Your dad and I had private little jokes that would cause us to laugh until tears ran down our cheeks. He always thought I understood cars and how they worked, even though I many times showed him this wasn't so. One time he told me he didn't mind if I parked sideways in the garage or really close to the wall, but please never do them at the same time again. He had worked long and hard to get the car out of the garage. I thought I had done a good job of parking. I think he exaggerated a little! It has been said some people don't park cars, they just abandon them when they get to where they are going. Maybe that was how I parked the car that day.

One day he wanted me to tow the old army jeep we had to get it started. This wasn't a favorite thing for me to do as I wasn't sure just what to do. After I towed the jeep around the block and back into the driveway, he calmly but seriously said, everyone should be towed by you at least once in their life. I thought I had done a good job but half a block of towing had started the jeep engine. I never looked back to see him frantically waving for me to stop. I should have stopped so he could take the tow line off the car but I had towed him for another half block with the jeep motor working well. We laughed about it later as he began to understand my knowledge of cars and how they work. He didn't ask for a lot of help with towing after that.

Do you boys remember our red and white pickup with a camper shell. Dad had rigged up a device with ropes and pulleys from the ceiling of the garage with hooks to hang the shell on when he didn't need it on the pickup. One day he wanted to take the shell off the truck. He asked me to slowly drive out of the garage as he lifted the shell off the bed of the truck. He understood what needed to be done but I didn't so I did what he told me to do. He only needed it lifted high enough so the legs of the shell would clear the sides of the truck bed. Then I was to stop so he could get to the ropes and lift the shell the rest of the way. The truck was pointed out of the garage which was good as I don't back vehicles very well. He got in the bed of the truck and lifted the shell up onto his shoulders and told me to pull forward. I had not driven anything but an automatic shift for years. Well, there was a clutch, a steering wheel, a gas pedal and a gear shift on the floor to deal with. Thankfully there was also a brake pedal because I popped the clutch, Dad started running toward the tailgate with the shell on his back, wondering what he could do when he got to the tailgate. No problem! I slammed on the brakes as I was only about to hit the wall of the garage and knew that would not be good. Quick thinking on my part I must say.

I was so afraid that I had hurt him I got out of the truck as quickly as I could get it shut down. When I saw he was all right I started laughing for some reason. By then he was standing by me laughing too. We finally quit laughing when we were shedding tears. Nervous laughter I guess. When we both calmed down Dad looked at me and, very seriously again said, you are the only person I know that can lay a six inch patch of rubber in a garage. I don't think it was a compliment. But he was always very patient with me and never raised his voice, even when I put him in harms way with my driving knowledge or lack of.

Dad had learned to fish when he was just a young boy and always loved to go fishing any free minute he had. I would go along but my fishing experiences were at times less than pleasant. I would forget to watch where I was walking along a creek and step into holes up to my knees or fall into the water. I never broke any bones but had ample opportunities to do so while fishing. He taught you boys how to fish when you were old enough to hold a fishing pole so you liked to go with him when you weren't in school.

One day I declined his invitation to go fishing with him. Bill, you went with him and were only gone a short time and came home. I thought you both must have had wonderful luck to fill your limits so fast. Dad was a good fly fisherman and had been using flies that day. The wind had blown the fly back into his face and the fly barb caught on his cheek just under his glasses. When I saw what looked like a little bumble bee stuck to his cheek I reacted as I always did in emergencies. In my always calm, cool manner I immediately grabbed my car keys and started out the door to take him to the doctor. He wouldn't go and said he could take care of this with my help. He figured the doctor would have to give him a shot to deaden his cheek so he could work the barb through the skin and clip it off. Dad reasoned he could do this himself and have only one pain. He used an ice cube to help deaden the site and gradually worked the lure through the skin and cut off the barb, then pulled the rest back out of his skin. He told me later it didn't hurt very much. That was when he came to get me out of the car as I was sitting there waiting to rush him to the doctor. I wanted no part of him doing his own surgery. Bill, you watched him do this. You told me later that Dad was the toughest man you have ever known.

At the same time I thought men knew everything about fixing any and everything that needed fixed, be it a door, a wall, a car, any electrical item etc. I really put him through his paces trying to keep up with me and my ideas of what I thought he should know, because he was a man and men should be able to do all those man things, building a new room onto the house, foundation, wiring and all that stuff. Dad got it done and done right with lots of how to books and help from friends.

Your school activities were lots of fun for us, maybe not always such fun for you boys. Programs then were allowed to celebrate the true meaning of Christmas and Easter so were special, lots of time and effort being put into making them special.

Looking back I realized the word wonderful was never a part of my vocabulary. Only when I turned my life over completely to the Lord did the world and everything in it become wonderful. It is great to see clearly now and honestly say something is wonderful. People are truly wonderful, even though sometimes they are ornery or what the world calls bad. They too are God's children and in that, they are wonderful. I guess when I found the word wonderful I became wonder-filled and full of joy. I keep that feeling almost all the time. I can't say it is always so. I have bad days and try hard to just let my engine idle then, trying not to buy into gloom and doom. Try it and see if that works for you.

Being happy or not is our decision to make. We can take life as it is handed to us and decide to make the most of it and be happy in all we do or we can resent or hate what life hands us and be miserably unhappy. As I learned to enjoy the good in my life and look away from the bad I formed the habit of seeing humor in most everything. Of course humor makes me laugh, which causes me to be happy. At times I must be the only one seeing the humor in a situation as I get some strange looks from those around me.

Your marriages were special and we were happy for you and celebrated. Grandchildren's weddings have come along much too soon it seems to me, but have been full of love and laughter. I wish I had kept a journal of what each grandchild said when they were small. You two boys told us some classic things too. At times I had to wait for my eyebrows to come down from my hairline but it was always informational! Such wisdom from such small people always amazed us. Some thoughts you and your kids have had were so simple and yet so wise. Seen through the eyes of a child, life, if given a chance can be simple yet beautiful. So here I am remembering such happy times that are countless, joyful times that truly blessed me and knowing that the good has far outweighed the bad, unhappy times. For that I am so grateful and feel so blessed.

I wish all my family could know that peace, happiness and joy in their lives as well.

# Chapter 27

# More Great Times with the Family

I DON'T WANT YOU to think our lives were nothing but misery, illness and worry. We had such a great time of enjoying life as we could, however we could. Not having a lot of money, we enjoyed picnics, birthday celebrations, anniversaries and any excuse to celebrate. There were humorous times when we would laugh until we cried as I told you about in the last chapter. There were days of just living life in a normal way without anything exciting happening. Thankfully there have been more of those days than the "exciting" ones that caused us grief, fear and other scary feelings.

Life in a small town was pretty relaxed compared to life in cities. A big treat was to go Denver and shop in the stores, go to fast food places, visit the amusement parks and ride those scary roller-coasters, or just spend time with our family there. As you boys may remember, at home you could wander all over the town and hillsides and feel free and safe. You should remember the things you did that you should not have done. When you were little you couldn't figure out how Dad and I knew what you had been up to by the time you got home, especially when he was a state patrolman. People were more than happy to call us to tell us our kids had misbehaved.

One benefit of a small town was that everyone looked out for all the kids and weren't afraid to tell them to stop doing something they shouldn't be doing. We parents knew our children were safe when out and about. Many eyes were on you and willing to take care of you if you needed help. It is too bad that those days are no longer with us. You had your problems growing up, everyone does. It was hard for teens especially to understand that all their classmates were having problems of their own, different maybe but still hard to deal with. But you survived into adulthood and went on with your lives.

We adults also took it upon ourselves to educate the kids in manners and behavior when they needed a gentle reminder. One day when I was in front of the counter at the drug store waiting for the clerk, a young boy came up and shoved me aside as he pushed in front of me and leaned on the counter. He was about twelve years old. Without thinking I took him by his shirt collar, pulled him out of line and told him never to do that again, and lectured him on being rude. I don't know if it helped him but he never cut in line in front of me again. Of course we wouldn't dare do that today.

Do you remember the fishing trips on the Gore Pass. We had many good times doing that. Only one time did we decide to take our dog Blackie along. He had the most fun of all that day. He would jump into the streams and swim or run if it was shallow enough. He would jump back out as the water in the mountain streams can be really chilly all year long. And in the manner of dogs he would shake himself to dry off and we moved fast to stay out of his way as he did that. About the time Dad would find a good place that looked like there might be fish in it, along came Blackie and jumped in and scared any fish away. Dad finally said enough and we went home without any fish. Blackie didn't get to go fishing again.

He was the dog that came to stay overnight so Dad could see him. That was the way you brought him into the family, Bill. He had to be put down sixteen years later, having been a faithful pet for all those years. Larry, you had the job of taking him to the vet for that.

Dad also had the fun of taking two grandsons fishing one day. Chris and Jacob were about five and six years old and very energetic to say the least. When they came home Dad got out of the pickup, looked at me and said ever so seriously, that is the last time I will ever take them fishing by myself. He would get one's pole set with line in the water, go to help the other one and by then the first one had thought he had a fish and pulled his line out of the water. This was a continuing process all afternoon, the fish stayed safely in the stream, Dad was exhausted, but the boys had a great time fishing! These are the times we could look back on and laugh and think how blessed we were to have our families close by to take fishing or whatever we could do to entertain them.

One summer we had the five youngest grandkids for a week at our house. The older two were too busy to take part in this kid stuff. We planned something every day that would keep them occupied and entertained. One day we went for a trip through the woods on Gore Pass. Each was told to find a strong fallen tree branch that would make a good walking stick. When we got home Dad showed them how to take the bark off, sand down the wood, stain it and have a walking stick. It was interesting to see how each picked a branch, some wanted huge branches they could hardly carry. Others took little ones that were too small. Eventually they all equaled out though. I think some still have their walking sticks.

One day we had a painting session after we all went out and found rocks to paint. We told the kids the parable of the first stone and they then each painted 1st on a stone to take home and one for Dad and me. I hope the lesson on judging others has stayed with them through life.

I have lots of special memories from the day of our marriage until today. Even with all the bad things that happened along the way there are so many good things and blessings they overcame the bad ones.

## Chapter 28

# *Recognizing Miracles*

Definition of a miracle: an event that appears unexplainable by the laws of nature and so is held to be supernatural in origin or an act of God.

I have been talking about a lot of bad things for most of this book to impress you that everyone has their share of troubles, heartaches and woes. I promised not to preach but I hope by now as you have read this far that you have received the message that without God in my life I would not have survived as well as I have. Many hard times and lots of serious illnesses have been overcome because I let the Lord help me. I could have said no to His help any time I chose. Death has been close too many times to not recognize the beauty of life. No where in the Bible are we told we are to have an easy, happy, wonderful life all our days. The Lord says He will be with us always, through all things, to the end of the age. His helping hand eases the pain, sorrow or any misery we go through. His willingness to love us when we are our most unlovable is a big miracle to me! I have a friend who thinks this is all a test of some kind!

I will tell you of miracles I have seen and experienced in my life and there have been quite a few. Many people have seen or experienced one or more. Some say if we dig deep enough into our memory banks, we can even remember before birth in the womb and our birth itself. I haven't gone into that remembering, if it is possible, or talked to anyone who has. I have read of it though and keep an open mind about this subject.

We tend to be blind to the miracles around us we call nature after a short time of admiring the beauty of them. It is said a coincidence is merely God's way of remaining anonymous. This is why we so often don't see the hand of God in our lives but prefer to call things we can't explain a coincidence. That also helps us to not have to deal with a God who we might fear, or hate, or just don't want to have anything to do with.

I am going to tell you about things and events that step outside the rules of nature as we know them, events that fit into the above description. Most have happened to me personally and some include your dad or center around him. He too knew something out of the ordinary happened to him at times. Some were recognized at the time they happened and others needed hindsight to understand the extraordinary events. These are what I call the "biggies" and are not necessarily in the chronological order in which they occurred.

The beauty of the mountains in Colorado, especially in early spring when life starts growing after a long winter, is wonderful and very welcome. This miracle happened on such a day when the air was clear and clean, just warm enough to not need coats but the newness of life hadn't turned into the hot days of summer. We were invited by Dad's Aunt Mary and Uncle Whitie to a fish fry. The local Rod and Gun Club hosted these picnics and furnished the trout which was cooked over a camp fire. Every one brought other dishes to share. After the long winter folks were anxious to be outside and a crowd of between twenty five to forty people came to enjoy the good time. The site was outside of town in an open space at the edge of the forest named Trout Creek camp ground. In those days a permit wasn't necessary to picnic there or even camp overnight.

You, Billy, were fourteen months old and wanted to go fishing like the big guys. I found a little trickle of water, perhaps one inch across and barely enough to call it a trickle. I gave you a little stick to pretend you were fishing and walked back to the group of people talking and laughing. I was as dumb as a post about little kids and didn't know how fast and far you could travel. It wasn't but a few minutes later that I heard you call "Momma" very calmly and then call again. I heard this over the noise of all those people talking. As I turned I saw you weren't where I had left you but heard you again quietly and calmly call "Momma". I somehow knew where you were although I couldn't see you. I ran opposite to where I had left you. You had fallen into an irrigation ditch and were only visible when I got to the edge of it, right over you. You were lying on your back with just your face out of the water, holding onto a weed with one hand, calmly calling me. I had to lie down on the bank to reach you. I didn't have time to call for help so I just did what I had to do and pulled you out of the water. You were down deep enough that I had to be careful not to fall in too. Only by God's grace and help did I get to you over the noise of the large group laughing and talking, no one else noticing anything wrong. Had I not found you, you would have washed down the ditch into the creek that ran fast close by and could have drowned before you were missed. I *heard* you call in my head as I could not have heard your quiet voice over all the noise. You never yelled loudly as no one else heard you. We left the picnic, too frightened by that close call to enjoy the day.

At the time we didn't recognize that I was helped by angels, the Lord, both or someone He had sent. I wasn't well acquainted with the idea of God being present in our lives. If we had understood and tried to explain to others we would have been thought to be a little "off the mark" of sanity. I know now the Holy Spirit or an angel saved your life that day, made me hear you calmly call me, showed me where you were and helped me to act fast enough to get you out of harms way. It was also a lesson in how much trust our children have in us to keep them safe. You seemed to know I would come for you. You weren't at all scared or excited, just very calm and very wet.

I don't know if this next story qualifies as a miracle or another type of gift from God. A few years after this when we now had both of you boys, we were traveling over Gore Pass to visit our families. Colorado is beautiful in the winter as well as other seasons but travel can be dangerous.

In those early days a mild recession was happening. We had to buy retread tires for our car. I don't know if those are even available anymore as they weren't the safest tires but were the cheapest. They weren't the snow tread tires we have today.

We were only about forty miles from our destination but the roads were a solid sheet of ice and had been for miles. Having you boys in the car with us always made me nervous and after a few hours on icy roads I was a nervous wreck. I knew if I said anything or cried, which I was about to do, it might distract Dad from his driving. He was an excellent driver and had not given me any reason to be so afraid. I was still afraid of everything in those days. I was not well acquainted yet with the idea of God looking out for us but I decided to pray for calmness and peace. I hardly had time to finish that short prayer and I was calm with all fear gone. A door had been opened that I had not known of before. Another nudge in my life's journey to finding the Lord.

Since that time I have never been afraid on icy roads, unless I'm driving but that's another story. We made it to our destination and home again safely. At the time I knew my prayer had been answered but didn't realize what a gift it was until years later. Once we conquer a fear through prayer and get the Lord's answer we don't have to deal with it again unless we make the mistake of allowing that fear to rule us. Common sense fear is useful in that it keeps us from making the mistake of walking in front of a moving truck or train, or making poor decisions that will harm us in some way. To let unreasonable fear rule us stifles our ability to enjoy life and live to our fullest abilities.

Both of you boys were in elementary school when the next miracle happened. Catherine, mother of your good friend Charlie who is our godson, and I decided it would be a good idea to get you three boys swimming lessons at the pool in Hot Sulphur Springs where there was a qualified instructor. The alternative for learning to swim was the Colorado River which runs close to town and not a good place to swim. Catherine and I carpooled for several weeks that summer for the lessons. Some days I would get in the pool although I am not a good swimmer and grow panicky if the water is over my head.

This particular day I had been in the water but got out on the bathhouse side of the pool. Just as I got out I heard you, Billy, calling "help" very calmly, then again "help" as you surfaced the second time. As I turned to find you, you were on the opposite side of the pool in seven foot deep water. I don't know how I got into the water. I didn't know how to dive but somehow I got to you. I had no idea of life saving techniques in water, was in way over my head, and had to save my son!

I don't remember taking time to pray but just grabbed you as you came to the surface again and dogpaddling, told you to hold your breath as we both went down. I had a hold on you, how I don't know, and pushed off hard from the bottom. As we surfaced I threw you through the air into shallow water. You must have weighed between forty or fifty pounds then. I couldn't have picked you up off a dry floor, never mind throwing you anywhere.

I went under again. As I came back up my fear of deep water started to grab me but I managed to swim to the shallow water where you were standing. When I say I swam it was more like beating the water into a froth and kicking enough to stay afloat.

We walked over to poolside and got out. When I asked you why you were in that deep water you said you thought it would be good to practice diving off the board in the deep end. However the instructor was busy with a new class and neither saw you dive nor heard you call for help.

I had big help that day and as happens when that kind of help comes, things got a little fuzzy. I don't remember some parts and didn't that day but some of it is still crystal clear. I don't swim anymore and you have a fear of water that you are working to overcome.

There were people sitting on the sidelines and I wondered what they might have thought of all this but I didn't go back to the pool to ask. Did they know they had witnessed a miracle.

## Chapter 29

# A Close Look at Death By Car

In our young days traveling by car wasn't nearly as hazardous as it is today. Speed limits weren't as high and people wouldn't travel as fast as they do now. We didn't have seat belts and kids stood up in the back seats or played on the floorboards or whatever kept them happy. As faster cars became available it didn't seem important, people were expected to drive in a safe manner. Today it is a risk to one's life to leave your driveway, especially since the advent of cell phones, vehicles with TV and other distractions.

Some of our more hazardous incidents occurred while in a car, with good endings fortunately.

In a dream I had Dad and I was saving someone in a car and it was important to know that angels were on the car helping us. After that dream when we were traveling out of town in a car I prayed a short pray asking that angels would be on the front of the car. That is one of the smarter things I have done.

Dad and I were on a trip to Nevada to visit family. It was the middle of the day, we were on Highway 80 in Utah, going up a long hill with twos lanes, with a passing lane between them. There was a gentle curve to our left but it was open with nothing blocking our sight. Dad had pulled into the passing lane, which was for up hill use only, to pass a gasoline tanker in the right lane. When we traveled I usually looked at scenery and didn't pay attention to the road, leaving the driving to Dad.

Suddenly all I could see out my window was the rear dual tires of the tanker and they were getting closer rapidly. I turned to see what Dad was doing. He was slowing down to try to get back behind the tanker. He had pulled over as closely as he dared to the tanker which gave me a good view of the underside of the tank and those big tires. As I looked at Dad I saw a pickup truck coming right at us. It had stock racks (upright boards on the side of the bed of the truck which gives more height to accommodate bigger loads) and it was loaded above them and above the top of the pickup. I can still see the driver, a woman with a round face, blondish hair down to her shoulders and great big blue eyes. She was close enough by then that I was able to see her this clearly. I could also see she was frozen at the wheel. She apparently had not shifted down to a lower gear to compensate for the load on her vehicle.

Her speed increased due to the steepness of the road. She didn't move or make any attempt to turn her vehicle which was being pulled into our lane by the centrifugal force on her overloaded truck. When something like this happens time seems to slow down. As Dad and I talked afterward we both thought we were going to die. We knew we were going to be hit head on.

The woman in the pickup didn't move but her truck did. It just seemed to slide sideways and cleared our car by about two feet. She didn't turn her steering wheel. If she had it may have caused her truck to turn sideways and hit us anyway. The whole truck just moved over and missed us. It moved like you would take a toy and shove it aside.

As this happened I was as frozen as she was. As I looked at her she never moved at all. Had she hit us we would likely have been shoved into the tanker truck which we were still running beside. That would have a caused a horrendous wreck for all of us.

After we got over the scare and started talking about what had happened we had to laugh about a tanker driver wondering what he had just witnessed. It took some time though before we could relax. We thanked the Lord as we knew He had either intervened Himself or sent the angels I always asked for when traveling. I have often wondered what that woman thought when she finally got slowed down enough to know she had missed dying too!

We didn't let fear overcome us but became more aware that something can happen so fast we don't have time to save ourselves. I don't know why we were spared then. What more can I say.

By the way this was the middle of summer with dry roads, no ice or snow or rain. Nothing for her truck to slide sideways on.

# Chapter 30

## A Miracle of Healing

After the awful incidents of shootings I talked about earlier, our lives had settled down to a normal pace. Having had poor health a good deal of my life, I had learned to live with a constant feeling of nausea, a lot of sessions of flu and most childhood diseases. It wasn't pleasant but didn't interfere too much with what I wanted to get done. I was working at the school as secretary to the superintendent of schools and also was the district bookkeeper. I enjoyed this job so much for a year or so I felt guilty taking pay!

You boys were growing up nicely and Dad was working for the Department of Highways, state of Colorado. We bought a house and worked on remodeling it. All was well. We still didn't go to church as I had put God on the shelf when the bad things happened, saying I would take care of my family myself if that was the best He could do! I was super mom indeed and controlled my environment as much as possible and tried not to be too harsh about it.

In my late thirties I began to feel something was going

on with my body that wasn't right but not bad enough to see a doctor. What started as fatigue I blamed on too much work at school and home, one day turned into a real disease. What started as a little round spot on my left upper arm that itched and hurt soon caused the skin to become hard and spread to the upper right arm. Several months of this that the local doctor couldn't diagnosis finally sent me to a doctor in Denver. He did a skin biopsy that came back showing the autoimmune disease scleroderma. The common name for this is hard skin. The skin on my upper arms was hard as wood. Then my fingers became involved and I started losing the ends of them and all sense of feeling was gone. I also started to develop what is called fish mouth which pulls your lips into something resembling a fish's mouth. Before that I had a wide smile but it soon became almost impossible to smile at all. I still today don't have the smile I once had because of the disease. I only became aware of this happening when one day Dad asked me why I never smiled anymore. I wasn't aware that I couldn't smile until then.

When the doctor told me what was wrong, he also said there was no cure but told me to come back in a month or so if it got worse. Just before my fortieth birthday I decided this aging thing was the cause of it all but maybe something should be done about it. I went to a different doctor in Denver who ordered a muscle biopsy. This too came back with a scleroderma diagnosis. I was hospitalized at this time and a young intern walked into my room, dropped that news on me and gave the good word that if the disease went systemic I might have a year to live if lucky and walked out of the room. Two groups of radiologists, surgeons and I don't know how many more doctors came up with the same diagnosis, the news that there was no known cause and no cure for this stuff. So I would have to make do. I was numb with fear, anger and pain.

My sister Norma came to the hospital to visit me and when I said, why me she answered why not you. That made me aware that if someone had to have this I would rather it be me than one of my family or friends. Yet I was devastated. All our plans were gone. The first week at home I sat and cried and felt sorry for myself, then decided that wasn't getting me anywhere so I got up and went back into the routine of life.

After the diagnosis I had swallowed my pride, called on God, saying Help! You know what, He was right where I had left Him and came to help me deal with the situation. But still not knowing differently I told Him I will bear this latest cross you have given me. I will be strong and stay cheerful, stiff upper lip and all that. Being a martyr was becoming a habit with me. I didn't know we can ask God to heal us, I just knew that I was being punished because I was guilty of something, anything. Why else would this happen to me.

Over a period of time the disease did go systemic and caused many stays in the hospital, sometimes in ICU when it affected my heart and intestines. The pain at times was unbearable. The heavy narcotic Demoral would take the edge off but not hold it for long. It is so addictive the doctor didn't give it often. .

During one hospital stay our priest, Father Chap

Cranmer, brought me *Healing* by Francis McNutt to read. As I read that book I was amazed to find I could ask God to heal me of this illness. What a revelation! But would the Lord know my voice. I had turned from Him in anger. Would He be able to see beyond guilt I had carried for so many years about everything that had happened in my life even though not my fault, would I have to confess before I asked Him to heal me. One question after another went through my mind. This was such a shocking, new idea that it took time to think it through. When I finally dared to begin to pray it was pretty scary. What if He said no, what if there were conditions that I couldn't meet. I wrestled with the whole idea for a while then decided there was nothing to do but jump in and ask Him to heal me. My prayer suggested if not complete healing, every little bit of help would be appreciated! My need to surrender my will to the Lord never entered my mind. After all, this healing thing was hard enough to take hold of right then.

At first I just begged Him to let me die, still trying to control. I gradually began to ask for the courage and strength to live with the disease and to help me get through the days as well as I could. I had a lot of pain during those years but was also able to keep working for six years. When the pain became too bad to bear my doctor would put me in the hospital and give me stronger pain meds than I could take on my own. I had to laugh when one young nurse told me when the pain got bad to call and she would come and shoot me up. That made me wonder what I would be getting but everything turned out all right.

The only treatment for the disease was large doses of

prednisone, up to sixty milligrams a day, which caused me over the months to swell up. I had a moon shaped face and I was so fat it would have been almost as easy to walk over me as around me. That was a miserable way to live.

Again I was told that if I didn't get total rest, freedom from all stress, I had less than a year to live. I asked the doctor what kind of choice that was but he just looked at me and said that was the way it was and to make a choice. This was after a thirty day hospital stay and I knew what the choice would have to be. I quit the job I loved having decided I loved life more!

I learned a lot about what is really important when you are living day to day not knowing what the next day would bring. What had been so necessary to be done perfectly no longer took precedence, rather getting it done at all had to be good enough. After two months of not doing anything other than taking care of my personal needs it was so nice to be able to dry the dishes one night for Dad. He was working full time and having to do all the housework and cooking too. I'm sure he was glad to finally see improvement. He never complained about all the extra work he had to do. I guess he knew the importance of just having him near me helped so much.

In the initial despair of thinking we are dying nothing penetrates a hard shell of disbelief, anger and pain. Physical pain makes death welcome, rather than months or years of this exquisite, shrill pain that death can make stop. It is a strange feeling to sit and just be, knowing there is nothing I can do to make a difference with this disease that is destroying my body. Prayers are ambiguous. Which way do I want it. A life of pain or release to a place I know is safe and real. So mostly I sat and waited—for what I didn't know. The darkness isn't always dark. It is lit by explosions of pain that would welcome darkness again. That is when I would beg God to let me die right now, don't wait another second. It is hard to learn to give over the control. Only once I considered suicide as I knew the pain was going to drive me quite mad and I didn't want that. I only touched on this idea a short while. I didn't want to have to explain to the Lord that I took His gift on the cross so lightly.

This stage of life brings a terribly numbing loneliness. It could be aloneness is a better word. A sense of complete aloneness no one is able enter into with me. Loved ones and friends stand by with all the offerings of comfort and love they have to give, which helps greatly. But they can only stand and watch, pray and hold me as I walk through this darkness on a path I do not understand, want or appreciate. They hold my hand but cannot enter into the despair, fear of the unknown, the lonely hours wondering what. Or when. Or why. They can entertain me or empathize with me but I am in a place they cannot come.

There were days I felt so totally alone except for knowing God was walking with me and giving me strength to do what I could do. I have never again had such a completely empty feeling, not necessarily despair but just a sense of being apart and withdrawing into myself. I suppose that was protection to not grieve for having to leave my loved ones so soon. I don't know. Only when numb disbelief gives over to surrender and acceptance do I find God in the desolation where I have no control, nor companions who truly know what I am going through. I finally empty myself enough to say "here I am Your will be done" to God and let go. I guess that is when the healing began. Amazing! It wasn't too long, maybe a week, month(s) that the darkness lifted and I was going to live and enjoy what time I had left, however long that might be. The darkness had turned into a reality of the world around me, no longer transparent but vividly, strongly real. Not of great importance but of great beauty. Time to enjoy what was real was a gift to take and fill to the top of the days ahead.

I began to see beauty and wonder in everything, colors more brilliant than ever before, my sense of smell became so sharp at times it stung my nose to breathe in the air. The world took on a new look for me and I found a new way of seeing what had always been around me. This continues with me today even as I write this because I learned how to appreciate everything no matter how small or insignificant in our socially tuned out ways. For the first time in a long time I was comfortable talking to God and knowing He heard me and cared for me just as He cares for all of us, each and every one of us, no matter our circumstance.

During those years when I became able to do some activity I took painting lessons, oil and china painting. Those hobbies gave me something to do that wasn't strenuous and yet kept me from just staring at the walls. I was able after a time to start taking part in family dinners and other fun things.

Twenty years after the onset of the disease I was tested and told there was no trace of scleroderma in my body.

Even today when I give my medical history to doctors

they ask if I know how blessed I am. Oh yes! I know I caught a miracle of healing! I don't know how many people were praying for me all those years but many, as everyone passed the word on to their prayer chains and friends. My priest and his wife faithfully prayed daily for years. My family and friends prayed too. I don't know just when the complete healing occurred but the symptoms left after about twelve years from the onset of the disease.

As I write this it sounds a little dramatic but it really happened. I have tried to keep that way of seeing the world even now because it changes how we believe, how we act and react with people, how we can see that this creation is something so big and beautiful it couldn't happen by accident. As I look at the pictures from the Hubble Space Telescope, I know. Someone had a plan! Could that someone be the one we call God. I choose to believe so.

As I had a lot of time during those days I began to build my relationship with the Lord. It is always surprising that no matter what we throw at Him, He can handle it and still love us and forgive us our foolishness. All the fear of dying was replaced by the knowledge that if I died I was safe with the Lord and need not worry, just allow Him take care of me. Since that time I have never again thought about my death or fear it. I have put in an order for a nice, easy way to go if that counts for anything!

As I had all this time to think, listen and talk to the Lord, that's what praying is you know, I realized the reason I didn't want to go to church was because I was angry at Him. If I was to have a working relationship with Him I needed to let Him into my life, not on my terms but on His. No more, I'll call you if I need something, don't bother me unless you hear from me. Otherwise I would still be wandering around trying to manage things as I do so well! So back to church we went and found a wonderful, welcoming family to share our lives.

Autoimmune diseases sometimes travel in packs. I don't know when the rheumatoid arthritis started as the pain is somewhat similar to scleroderma. I have been treated now for that for thirty plus years. Medical science keeps coming up with new and better things to keep the RA from becoming totally crippling but it still impacts my body and life. Once again I give God the credit for my being able to stay mobile and active when it would be easier to give up and stay in bed. Doctors are some of the Lord's helpers too.

This chapter on miracles stands out as the biggie but many others come close.

# Chapter 31

## Angels May Be Near

Dad and I along with your son Shane had gone to Texas to celebrate Christmas with you and your family, Larry. We had a chance to experience one of their infamous ice storms on Christmas Eve. That was a first for me but since then I have seen the same condition outside my door on the street where I live.

On the morning of Christmas Eve I woke to see Dad sitting on the floor next to the bed. I couldn't get him up off the floor so called you and Shane to help. You managed to get him onto the bed but he was not well so we called for an ambulance. When it came the walk was so icy four people walked dad to the gurney parked next to the ambulance. The EMTs were afraid if the gurney got away from them on the ice Dad would wind up on the street. By the time he got to the hospital whatever was taking place had stopped and he was okay. He stayed in overnight for observation but came home for Christmas dinner.

He had had some episodes like this before and I would

have to call family or medics to help get him off the floor. He never complained about any pain with them. Hospital tests showed nothing because whatever was wrong had corrected itself and he was okay by the time he got there. I suspect the incident itself in some way affected his brain so he couldn't remember what was happening to him. These episodes did leave him feeling weak for a few days.

The day after Christmas we started home, Shane driving on a thick layer of ice and being very careful. When we stopped for gas Dad stepped out of the Jeep on the ice and immediately was on his back on the ground. He fell so hard it's a wonder he didn't break a bone or two. Shane and I tried to get him up on his feet but we too were slipping and sliding so badly we couldn't get any footing to lift him.

A pick-up truck pulled up behind us and two really big men came and asked if they could help us. They each took one of Dad's arms and easily lifted him to his feet and helped him back into our vehicle. We thanked them and they just smiled and walked away. Were they angels sent to help us. I don't know but they could have been. Things like this happen to people all the time and we aren't sure what is going on. These fellows were bigger than Shane who is good sized and they were strong enough to lift Dad as easily as I would lift a child. Shane and I couldn't help, there wasn't room. Those fellows filled all the space around Dad and they weren't sliding and slipping. Angels. I think so.

# Chapter 32

## Kayleen Herrama's Miracle

Over the years I have listened to many people tell of the miracles that have happened in their lives. Some are the kind that happens to us all, too many to call a coincidence. Remember what I told you earlier about a coincidence being God's way of remaining anonymous. Think about that for a minute. If every wonderful event that happened had God's written signature on it would we still be in awe of them. Would it become common place enough to say that's just God doing His thing again. Would it lessen the respect for those things He does.

We humans have such a short attention span that it takes a lot to impress us. We would just throw the miracle aside without thinking and wait for the next biggie to happen, assuming it is going to happen. Then what if it doesn't.

I have permission to print this story a friend told our study group several years ago. I tell it as she sent it to me and will add the fact about place and water conditions she doesn't mention. One fact is in the deep lakes in the Colorado mountains the water never gets very warm, even in the middle of summer. Most of them are fed by snow melt which adds to the temperatures staying cold. Swimming in them is only for the bravest and toughest who can withstand the cold, even close to shore.

Kay's story in her words. "A friend and I had gone for a boat ride on a lake in the Grand Lake area and ended going up the big Colorado River Bay. It was a beautiful September afternoon and as we neared a point we decided to go ashore to explore the woods there. I tied the boat down to a big rock. While we were hiking it looked like an afternoon storm was coming in. The wind was pretty intense so we headed back to shore. When we got to where we could see the boat, the wind had forced the knot loose and was blowing the boat out into the lake. The lake was deserted by now, we were in an area where there are no roads and this was before cell phones came into use. Without thinking, I ran down to the shore, jumped into the freezing water and started swimming across the bay, sort of panicked and not thinking ahead. I had all my clothes and my hiking boots on. I had a light jacket on as well as jeans and a warm shirt, dressed for that time of year.

I came to realize the wind was blowing harder than I could swim and was rapidly pulling the boat away from me. I honestly felt like I was not going to make it as this was way beyond my swimming ability. By this time I could not catch my breath. I thought that I would probably drown as I couldn't get back to shore either.

At this point I felt some unbelievable strength and

spiritual energy that seemed to lift me to the boat and I was able to climb on board and keep it from crashing into the rocks it was headed for. To this day I know this strength was sent from God. I have always believed in angels and can think of several instances where they protected and guarded me from danger."

And that is Kayleen Herrema's miracle that day.

# Chapter 33

## *Hearing God's Call to Act*

In Romans 7: 15 Paul asks why he does what he shouldn't do and knows he shouldn't do it but does not do what he knows he should. I can relate to that. As I think about it I have decided if Paul couldn't figure it out, I don't think I am capable of doing it either. I will just write about times that some would call instinct but I prefer to call a nudge from the Lord. Although I have heard Him speak to me in a still small voice, these are times that are more a mental push. Another of God's coincidences.

One of the important events or miracles came about when my mother, your Grandma Lou, was ill. Dad and I had gone to visit her and all the family living around her. She was living with her granddaughter Lula May as she was eighty eight years old and too frail to live alone anymore.

One day she complained that she really didn't feel well. She showed us her legs and she had the worst case of edema I have ever seen. From knees to ankles they were double in size and even a little more than that. We rushed her to her doctor who took one look at her and sent us straight to the hospital. After she was settled in and comfortable we went back to Aunt Nina's house for the night.

The next morning around ten, Dad, my sister Norma, my niece Lula May and I went to see Mom. We were in for a shock. As she lay there hyperventilating she was unaware we were talking to her. She had been like that for several hours already. The nurses had been trying to get her to breathe through her nose, exhale through her mouth. She simply didn't or couldn't hear them. She had oxygen on but it was useless as she was breathing through her mouth. I have wondered why they didn't put an oxygen mask on instead of the nasal canella but they may have tried that and she rebelled against it. Hour after hour the four of us worked with her to get her to breathe normally but nothing helped. She had what I called a death mask on her face, eyes staring past us into what, mouth wide open and panting for air. She never closed her eyes. After hours of this we four were also breathing in rhythm with her. At six p.m. a nurse told us Mom wouldn't live through the night. However we still continued to work with her, trying to slow her breathing, giving her back rubs and doing what we could to make her comfortable. We couldn't just sit there and watch her die without trying to help her. Once in a while she would act like she knew us and would say a few words then back to the endless panting for breath and staring into space.

It was in the wee hours of the next morning, around two. As I was looking out a window I was praying for her and asking God's will be done and if it was to be, that she be granted a peaceful and holy death. Quite suddenly and urgently I was "told" to baptize my mother. I had talked to her some years earlier about being baptized but she couldn't remember it ever happening. I didn't press the point then as I was still a little shy about pushing my faith on people. Now I'm being told to baptize my mother! We were in a strange city, I knew no priests or other clergy and I also knew Norma would resist me doing this. She would have made a scene and I didn't have time to explain to her what I was going to do.

I grabbed a basin, put water in it, got a towel and told mom I was going to baptize her. This is considered a "layman's" baptism and is done in emergencies without knowing if a baptism has been done previously. It is called a conditional baptism in our church. I did this without saying anything to anyone else. I did it so fast my sister didn't have time to react, my niece didn't understand and Dad would back whatever I felt was necessary. In about twenty minutes Mom resumed normal breathing, fell asleep and the four of us went to find a quiet place to rest for a while. At five thirty a.m. we all returned to her room. The day nurse was there and she was so surprised Mom was still alive, as they all thought she would die that night. Being told to go get breakfast we went to the cafeteria to eat, which took about forty-five minutes.

When we got back to the room Mom had had a bed bath, her breakfast and was sitting in a chair playing solitaire on her bedside table. She looked at us and said "where have you been."

We wanted to ask her where she had been but didn't! That episode was such a strain on her body that she had to be moved into a nursing home where she lived another three months.

One morning after a caregiver had wakened her and prepared her for breakfast she was fine. Thirty minutes later when breakfast arrived she was dead. From appearances it was a fast and easy death, either another heart attack or an aneurysm had ruptured. God's will for her was worked out in His time. To keep a record of her baptism, we had our priest in Kremmling put this information into the book of records at Trinity Episcopal Church.

Some time after the hospital baptism Norma told me how much she resented me doing that. She didn't have a good reason for it except she had always wanted to be the boss or center of the action. Fifteen months later we got an invitation to attend her baptism. She had been in AA for years and talked to God all the time but something she saw that night changed her idea of her relationship with Him. She saw a miracle of healing and knew there was more to life than just saying we believe. Perhaps that was what God intended to teach when He pushed me to do the baptism.

Dad's mother, your grandma Dorothy, had heard us tell this story about my mom. As her health started to fail I asked her one day if she had considered baptism or had been baptized. She knew she had not been baptized due to the awful years of her growing up when few seemed to really care if she even existed, except to be their housemaid. She told us she would like to be baptized but couldn't get to the church anymore as her physical condition made her pretty much house bound.

When we three lived in Kremmling, Grandma

Dorothy had gone to church with us and enjoyed it. She liked Father John and he would call on her at times. She did comment that she didn't like sitting on those hard benches in church!

I talked to our priest who said she would arrange to do a home baptism, which she did. She and Grandma Dorothy sat together on a couch. Reverend Lou explained carefully what the rite was all about and that it would make her a member of Jesus' family. Grandma never once looked away. When questioned if she understood what she was about to do and what that meant, she knew exactly that this baptism was what she wanted and needed. Four of our family members were happy to be witnesses. We were so happy to see the look of joy on her face after the baptism. What a wonderful feeling of peace and God's blessing was with us all. Grandma's face was lit up and she smiled the biggest smile she had to give. Soon after that it became necessary to move her into an assisted living facility and then into the nursing home where she spent the rest of her life.

Reverend Lou continued to call on her. The home's chaplain wasn't as welcome for some reason. She didn't give him much of her time. Only Grandma Dorothy knew why and she didn't say. She enjoyed Lou's visits very much. They helped her understand what was happening to her and that she was in the Lord's care. She was ready to be with the Lord. She didn't say it like that, she would say she couldn't live like she was forced to live and hated it. I think she felt comfortable knowing the Lord was waiting for her.

One day she had showed us a little girl standing at the foot of her bed and wanted me to give her a drink of water. I went along with this and acted out giving someone a drink. Grandma immediately told me I wasn't doing anything and called the little girl to her bedside so she could help her. Was this an angel or just a hallucination. I don't know. The last few weeks she had regressed to where she no longer knew she had a son, which hurt Dad but he could understand what was happening. When we would visit her, he was Uncle Whitey and I was Aunt Mary. (They were the aunt and uncle who raised Dad and had helped raise Dorothy.) She would tell me to feed Uncle Whitey if her dinner tray was there and I couldn't fool her by pretending to do it. She would tell me I wasn't doing anything and to stop, so I would. She didn't know who I was but I couldn't fool her with my make-believe actions.

On the day she died Dad and I were with her. We weren't told what had happened to cause her to be unable to speak or open her eyes and we were too upset to think to ask at the time. Her illness over the months had paralyzed her from the waist to her feet so it may have spread to all of her body. Although she couldn't speak or open her eyes she would scrunch up her eyes in response to what we would say to her. She was at peace and there was no stress in her. I think she was already seeing the waiting messengers who would take her home, or maybe even Jesus himself. I don't know who or what but she was ready and waiting to go with them. Dad and I sat with her talking and singing to her. She was at peace but was also hanging onto life.

Dad left the room for a minute and I took that time to talk to her and tell her it was okay to go on, that we understood and knew she would be taken care of by the

Lord. She scrunched her eyes to let me know she heard me but still continued to hold on. When I left the room shortly after that, Dad also told her it was okay to go with the angels when they came for her, that he loved her and knew she would be in a better place with the Lord. She again scrunched her eyes to let him know she heard and understood what he said. She'd had a half dose of pain meds at three p.m. Her regular dose was given at six p.m. Shortly after that she gently slipped away. We both were with her.

It is such an amazing thing when someone is alive and breathing and in the next second is gone. I have seen this happen several times now and never get used to how fast life stops. One breath and then none. I guess a lesson would be don't wait to make peace with your loved ones, you might not get the chance to do so. Getting to know the Lord a little earlier might be a good idea too. I don't have any idea what happens but after reading books regarding dying and being with those who are dying, I know something wonderful takes place.

Trust me when I say this as I have gone from being terrified of death in my early years to seeing my loved ones go on to a better life in a peaceful, calm manner. Don't think I am telling you that the grief and loss isn't real and terribly hard to get through. I have been there too many times and know there are days when living seems impossible. But as a friend told me when Dad died, it doesn't get better, it just gets easier to deal with. Time eventually lets us learn to take deep breaths again.

# Chapter 34

## A Call to Ministry

One of what I would think of as miracle in my life is when I was called to be a minister of healing prayers. Here is that story.

I almost left this part of my life out of the book but realized I would be denying the gift God had given me. We use the words intercessor or healer to shorten calling it by a more pretentious name such as one who heals. That is, we are vehicles or pipelines open to the Lord to ask for the needs of people to be taken care of by His healing power. I avoid the word channel as it carries a weird connotation in too many peoples' minds. By whatever name you choose to call it, it is a spiritual side of God's will for us to be healthy people. I think everyone can pray like this but so many are too timid to try.

In 1991, after completing a four year Education for Ministry class I briefly considered becoming a deacon. That didn't feel right so I forgot about that ministry. Ignoring for years a feeling of being called to be a minister to pray for healing of people, in 1997 I finally talked to my priest about it. We set up a schedule of prayer time and I started reading all the materials I could find by others who had this ministry of praying for healing for people. After a year of reading those books plus books about the saints who had special gifts I told my priest I could not read one more serious book. She told me to read a good novel which I did and that gave me a break from the serious stuff. Many prayers for discernment finally brought the answer and we felt the call was real. So I stepped out in faith to develop a ministry offering prayers for healing for people.

I started out timidly at first, praying with people after Communion on Sundays. I was still trying to find the best way this praying should be done and more or less winging it. I had attended many teaching seminars and even worked with those who prayed for others. I had some idea how these special prayers should be offered but didn't want to do anything to cause anyone harm using wrong words.

One Sunday a young man came to me with the problem of lung cancer. He was only in his mid twenties and newly married. He had growths in his lungs that doctors had determined to be cancerous. He was told this news on Friday and came for prayers on Sunday. I was uncertain how to proceed but remembered that is was best to rebuke the cancer or whatever the illness was, in the name of Jesus and send that illness to Jesus to deal with. This is necessary so that the illness doesn't stay some place near by or go into someone else. In Matthew 12 we are told that rebuked evil or an illness will go into an arid place and will return to the place from which it is sent unless it is sent to Jesus. If it does return and finds a clean home it goes in and brings seven other spirits with it. I have paraphrased the Bible text and suggest you read it in full. Several people were praying with me during this time. On Tuesday, two days later, I got a call telling me that the doctors were astounded as there was no sign of any cancerous growths in his lungs.

Some years later this young man returned for healing prayers, the problem with his lungs had occurred again. After we had prayed for him he went to his doctor and once again tests showed nothing in his lungs. His doctor remarked about not understanding what was happening but knowing his patient's contacts and prayers he would have to say he knew something unusual had happened. Yes indeed, Jesus happened!

A short time later a group of folks joined in this ministry as they too felt this was something they were called to do. As a group we attended a three day workshop of the National Order of St. Lukes in Wyoming. We heard many stories regarding healing services, training sessions and other workshops and prayer sessions but they would make this book too long.

When we returned we started a separate service of healing in the evenings and soon were doing two a month. During the early days our bishop gave me permission to anoint people with holy oil that he had blessed. This in itself was a gift as bishops don't give too many people this privilege. I know people can buy oil in religious stores but it has not been blessed as special healing oil. I might add it caused some clergy to resent me as they felt only clergy should have this privilege.

At times I invite the Holy Spirit to join us in a way we can know and be sure of. This is usually manifested by a feeling of electricity going through my hands into the person I am praying for. They too feel this power. Sometimes the Spirit takes over totally and the one being prayed for will be what was once called being slain in the Spirit. I prefer the term resting in the Spirit as it sounds less threatening. You may have seen this happen on TV shows or in your own church. Some may be false but I assure you most are real. It is not a dog and pony show to impress people or shouldn't be used in that way. The only time I touch people is to hold either one or both hands. I never push them or touch their heads and only will place a hand on a bad back or some other place of pain. I have been prayed for and pushed until it was either sit down or be pushed down. I am aware of how healing prayers should be offered. It isn't a physical contest to see who is strongest. Those people are trying to use their own power to obtain the results they want.

When the Spirit moves it isn't necessary for me to do anything but pray. When the resting takes place the person is awake and hearing the noise around him or her but is unable to move or speak until the Spirit has finished His work in them. There is nothing frightening or dangerous in this, but a blessing of inner healing which we need as well as physical healing.

The same feeling occurs when we pray and the Spirit or Jesus or God answers us. I am not sure which of the Trinity answers but we are in a place of silence and hear only someone speaking. When the answer is complete we are free once again to continue with whatever we were doing.

In 1 Corinthians 12 we hear about gifts of the Spirit which I guess come from the Holy Spirit. There are several gifts. Some people get wisdom, some a gift of healing, others a gift of tongues, one may receive the ability to discern spirits and there are more. Read about them with open eyes and open mind.

Along with the healing gift I also received the gift of tongues which I call my prayer language. This gift is greatly misunderstood by most people. It once was thought that if you didn't speak in tongues you weren't a true Christian. Nonsense! This gift can be misused. It is not used to control the Spirit or God. Generally we pray in tongues when we pray with anguish too deep for words letting the Spirit pray for us. It certainly should never be used to show off your gift or as a way of amusing people. It is a holy gift and should be treated with respect.

What we feel is a physical need or illness may be more connected to emotional or spiritual conditions that need tending to. We had been praying for several months for a lady with advanced lung cancer. Because it didn't seem Jesus would heal her I had the nerve to challenge Him and ask why. He didn't answer me but she did. One evening after our healing session she told me very quietly, Mona, there are more ways to be healed than just physically. I have been healed emotionally and spiritually and I am no longer afraid to die. Then I could understand the prayers had been answered the way Jesus chose to heal her. She lived a few weeks after that but died with peace in her heart and mind.

As I have prayed with others over the years as well as finding it true in my own life, it became apparent that the lack of trust and belief in God, the unwillingness to bend our will to His can block His healing power. It is a big step in faith to say to the Lord, I trust you and whatever you are doing in my life. I would share more with you but as all this ministry is done with complete confidentiality I can't give too much information so I don't breach the privacy of people I pray for. I try not to retain any information as this is between the person prayed for and Jesus. The group praying is merely a pipeline for them to connect with each other. Everyone can pray for themselves but some people like to have an intercessor lift up their needs and concerns. That is what the prayer ministers do for them. Nothing mysterious or spooky about it but a spiritual gift we are to share.

I pray all the time for people's needs but seldom remember to pray for my own illnesses. One day I had to been out in a terrible wind storm and later developed a headache, ear ache and the whole right side of my head including my scalp was sore to the touch. The next day I was still having some pain but had doctored myself without too much success. About 2:00 p.m. I was sitting quietly reading and suddenly my nose started to bleed. It ran so hard nothing I could do would stop it. After an hour or more of pinching my nose and various other treatments it finally stopped. About 5:00 p.m. as I sat reading the bleeding started again. It went on until I started to get light headed and was considering calling for help to go to the hospital. That didn't appeal to me as I know one way they stop this is to cauterize and that doesn't sound like fun.

It came to me that I could pray for myself like I prayed for others. Well, duh! I simply said, Jesus please heal my nose of whatever is making it bleed. Please stop the bleeding. The bleeding stopped instantly. It took me a few minutes to realize there was no more blood. I had been healed right then as soon as I asked. I did remember to thank Him! My nose was quite sore for a few days from being pinched so hard but it too recovered. I don't know what caused this problem as it hasn't happened again. I blamed it on being in the wind causing an allergy.

I have, through this ministry, witnessed many miracles of healing by the Lord. I chose to include this in this section to include those miracles.

## Chapter 35

# Aunt Nina's Miracle

Years ago when my sister Nina worked at the hospital where you boys were born, she witnessed a miracle of healing. She wasn't a professed Christian but had thoughts and questions about God and Jesus at times that led me to believe she wanted to know what it was all about. She wasn't sure just what she had seen and didn't ask anyone to explain it, only told us about it.

At that time the coal mines were still operational and many times men would be injured. She was a licensed practical nurse. In those days in small hospitals, registered nurses weren't that common in rural Colorado. The doctors would train LPNs to assist in any way needed so she got to help in surgery, the delivery room and in the emergency rooms as well.

On this day she was working the day shift when a man was brought in from an accident in a mine. X-rays showed six ribs broken loose from the spine, three on each side. So many years ago there were no emergency flights for life to send him to Denver so the doctor had him admitted, put to bed, gave him medications for comfort and made arrangements to have him taken to Denver the next morning. This was called stabilizing and preparation to transport. Several of the man's family and friends stayed the night with him and prayed without ceasing. They also brought his pet dog which was a Doberman or some big guard type dog. The staff was afraid he would bite them as they took care of their patient! However he slept under the bed all that night and didn't bother them. Perhaps he knew they were helping his master.

The next morning when the doctor and Aunt Nina went in to get the patient ready to move to Denver the man said, no need to ship me anywhere, I am fine and want to go home, or words to that effect. After a debate between patient and doctor, the doctor agreed to take another set of X-rays. To his and Aunt Nina's surprise there were no ribs broken from the spine, everything was just as healthy as it should be. As they looked at the two sets of X-rays side by side they were at a loss to understand. They helped the fellow get dressed and he, his family and dog went home and he lived a long life. I would add that they were all of the Christian Scientist faith.

Your aunt Nina told us about this as everyone in town knew something extraordinary had happened, so no privacy was broken. She saw the X-rays of ribs broken away from the spine one afternoon and then saw the X-rays the next morning when the ribs were connected to the spine as they should be. If some people had told me this I would have doubted them a little but Aunt Nina wasn't given to making up stories and was so totally amazed by it all we knew that she had witnessed a miraculous healing. She knew it too.

# Chapter 36

## Talking to the Lord

I WILL PROBABLY WRITE this several times over as I remember special thoughts and quotes, answers to prayer, so I must start this part of my story somewhere and now is as good as any.

I don't know just when I became aware of prayer outside church services where everyone prayed the Lord's Prayer together or said amen to the minister's prayers. Something had to have made me aware that personal prayers are available and heard but also necessary for us to stay in touch with the Lord in person, not just in a group.

Paraphrasing Peter Wagner's book, *Prayer Shield,* he says we pray to God to make it possible for Him to do something whereas He wouldn't enter into it otherwise. He doesn't just step into our lives at His will although He could. We need to ask, to invite Him in so He may act.

I have heard this said in another way, that God is polite and would not push Himself into our life unless we invite Him. If we want His help we need to invite Him into the situation. This then is why we pray. There are so many kinds of prayer, formal worship, prayers groups, individual prayers of thanksgiving, petitions on others' behalf, foremost of course prayers of praise. We often forget to thank Him and recognize what He has done and is doing for us. The order of the Lord's Prayer puts praise first, asking His will be done, asking for our own basic needs to be filled along with others needs, forgiveness for and recognition of our sins or trespasses as we forgive others. That part is really tough to pray as we seldom forgive others as we would like God to forgive us. We finish with more acknowledgement of His kingdom, power and glory forever.

We don't have to be this formal in our personal prayers but I try to remember to at least thank Him for the day's gifts and life at some place during praying. Sometimes it is just thanks for this day. I tend to wander through many places in prayer so I just try to cover all the bases during the day. I also use what was once called "jet" prayers which are one or two words on behalf of someone or something when immediate prayer is needed and time is short. This works when a person's name comes across your mind, a one line prayer "Lord, be with _________" is all that is needed to hold that person up for the Lord's action. Details not necessary. You may not know them anyway, but something prompted you to pray for that person. Do it then as the prompting you got means it is important for a prayer to be said right then.

In a conversation with one of our priest's I said I talked to God just like I talked to him. He said, tell me that's not true. I laughed and told him it was so. I never was rude to him anyway and I think he was just joking. I hope that is so. I try to be careful when praying not to use words that would offend Him. But even when I was most angry with the Lord I still maintained enough respect to just tell Him to go away and leave me alone, I would call Him if I needed Him again. The Lord can handle anything we can say to Him including our rage and bitterness. However, I don't think it wise to be a smart mouth. When I in anger told him something to the effect I could do as well as He had done in a bad situation, I was telling Him to go back to being a distant God. I didn't resort to cursing at Him. Please don't use His name as a swear word either. God's last name is not damn.

I have heard so many times that God can handle anything we can throw at Him and still love us as one of His own. Wouldn't it be nice if people could do that.

When I am distressed about something or someone, usually a family member or friend's crisis, I try to find a quiet place to sit and talk to the Lord about it. I ask Him to intervene if needed to calm a situation or someone but then I wait to hear what He might say, if He will give me a hint what I might do to help. Sometimes it is to make a gift of enough money to pay the rent this month or some other mundane thing. Often it is to call or send a card to let people know I am thinking of them and available to do what I can to help. I don't offer advice unless asked. We are not Solomon but can suggest ways if we know them and are asked to help. I am not a professional counselor, a member of clergy or otherwise trained in helping in this way. Neither are most of us. Usually the best we lay people can do is just listen to them, pray with them and let them know the Lord hears them, loves them and will help in His way in His time. A gift of food is always welcome when someone is ill or too distraught to cook.

There is a method of praying called centering prayer which can be done alone or in a group. The format is easy to follow and the purpose is to become still, clear our minds of daily stuff and listen to what the Lord may say to us. This can be preceded by reading a Psalm or a verse or two from Scripture to put you in a place away from daily cares. It is a calming, peaceful way to pray. It takes a little practice to do it successfully as there are always outside noises that can distract us.

When I was in a group just beginning to center it seemed about the time I would become totally still the furnace would come on, a bird outside would get loud, or traffic on the street imposed itself. So it does take time and practice but is well worth the effort.

Once when I had stilled myself, breathing quietly and slowly, body at ease and comfortable, I saw in my mind's blackness, which is what you want, a distant cross which lasted only a second as we have learned to immediately clear all images away. Another time I was pleasantly surprised to see a beautiful brown eye right next to my face for just a second, an image of a gentle face came into view but was gone when I cleared it away. Another time a beautiful green cloud appeared in the distance.

I had started centering at home nightly instead of just once a week when the group met. Dad would answer the phone and I would close doors to achieve almost silence.

This had gone on several weeks and was a great way to close out the day's activities. However one evening as I centered quietly, an ugly fierce face came flying at me from off to the left of my vision and what should have been eyes were just red, hate filled holes. Well, it goes without saying I opened my eyes looked around and that stopped my centering while alone. I was afraid to try again while alone and when the group met again they prayed at length for me to be free of whatever had entered my space. I never have centered alone again though. That face was pure evil and from whence it came I know not but I don't want to encounter it again, especially since I am now alone in the house. Is that cowardly of me. I guess it is but I have seen evil's face twice now and heard its voice once so it isn't something I care to set myself up for again. I told in an earlier chapter about hearing the voice of evil challenging my belief in God while I knelt in church. These incidents are not pleasant. It has been quite a long time since this happened so I might try centering prayer again, asking Jesus to sit with me while I do it. I would then be protected.

This is a good place to tell of the other time I saw an evil face. The occasion was an instructed Lenten meditation group. The leader would give us the lesson to mediate on and then we would quietly sit and write or just think of what it meant to us. We were sitting in a circle and as I happened to look up and across the room a person was looking back at me. I almost yelled out because the face I saw wasn't a human face at all, rather a characterization of one. It was long and distorted with no color to it, rather a white expressionless face with red eyes blazing with what appeared to be hatred, aimed right at me. The verse Jesus uses to describe the Pharisees as white washed tombs came to mind. I dropped my head and until the leader spoke again I was afraid to look up. When I finally did the person's face was quite normal and the meditation went on. This person was always nice to me and it surprised me to see this on her face.

In Matthew Jesus calls the Pharisees white washed tombs meaning beautiful on the outside but full of hypocrisy inside. This is a paraphrase so I suggest you read the verses for yourself. If anyone tells you there is no evil presence in this world don't believe him. I have seen it twice and heard its voice once. When it happens it will scare the hell out of you for sure! Literally! Which is good. Then you can let God into your life.

Don't try to impress God with beautiful phrases, wonderful images or other ways to tell Him how smart you are. He knows you and how you talk. He might not recognize your voice if you carry on at great length. Be yourself, be honest. Remember, He knows you better than you know yourself. There are people who have been given the gift of prayer. I have only known one person with this gift in all these years and only once did she pray in my hearing. She used words that are used daily by all of us but in such a way that it was beautiful to hear. The praises rolled off her tongue in such tones that everyone started breathing very softly so not to miss a word. It was truly a remarkable prayer and I wish I could hear one like it again.

When we pray we also need to stop talking and listen to Him. If He chooses to speak to us, either aloud as happens to some or quietly within our mind, we will miss what He is saying if we are too busy telling Him what we have to say. How He speaks to us is a mystery to me but I know His voice. The first time I heard it, whether it was God, Jesus or the Holy Spirit I don't know. I was taken by surprise and was unable to answer a question I was asked for a time. This I told you about when He asked me why I prayed for two children when I had three. All the times I have heard His voice I have also felt like I was in a sphere of silence and peace, never frightened. He doesn't use a lot of words, only saying what is necessary. When I answer, if an answer is needed, I might use more words than necessary but it takes a little doing to put my thoughts into words. If He wants an answer He wants an answer. I can only get back out of that silent place when He is satisfied with my answer. He is patient and doesn't ask me to hurry! I never feel uncomfortable once I realize what is happening, rather the peace and calmness is extraordinary. I would almost like to stay in that place! All the time this is going on I am awake and aware of everything around me but it is like it fades a bit and goes on without me.

The last time it has occurred I was watching TV one evening by myself. I could see the TV out of the corner of my eye as my attention had been drawn away from it a little. I couldn't tell you what was happening on TV. This was the time I was asked if I was willing to die for my faith. I guess that sounds a little strange but it has happened enough times that I recognize the feeling that comes with it. Then I just relax and go with it as I can't stop it. Once the conversation is done I feel relaxed and able to do what I was doing.

Many, many people have this happen and feel blessed as do I. Some say they hear a loud voice or almost a roar and they know to listen closely. Fortunately I hear a small, soft voice. Listen, listen, listen. He will never tell you to do something that will harm you or anyone else. He will never ask you to do something that will get you in any trouble with the law. He will never ask you, in any way, to act or be anything against His teachings. If the voice you hear does this it isn't Jesus or the Holy Spirit or God you are hearing. Shut that voice out fast.

I can't explain how or why or when God chooses to speak to us. I just know it happens, has happened to too many people over too many centuries to not believe it does happen. People have trouble accepting that others have gifts of the Spirit or witness miracles or hear the voice of the Lord. They may choose to think if it hasn't happened to them it isn't possible. Maybe it has happened to them and they didn't recognize what it was or from where it came. It pays to keep your eyes open and your ears tuned to things that might not be ordinary in your life. God keeps dropping little hints of His presence in this world all the time. You need to watch for them!

I want to mention a few verses of Scripture about praying that might make it clear for you to understand how important it is to pray.

In Matthew chapter 26 starting in verse 36 we learn about Jesus praying in the garden before he was arrested and then crucified. He didn't pray one time but several times. Jesus talked to God the Father many times during his ministry on earth. That is the biggest lesson telling us how important it is to pray.

In Luke chapter 18 verses 1 through 8 we hear about a persistent widow lady. She kept asking and asking. The lesson here is keep asking, sometimes one prayer isn't enough.

First Thessalonians chapter 5 we are told to rejoice always, to be happy in knowing the Lord, that His happiness far outweigh the world's idea of happiness. Be joyful in the fact that you know Him.

The little book of James is loaded with information for us. I suggest you read verse 13 in chapter 5. He says if anyone is sick pray for them. Since James is a short book why don't you read all of it.

## Chapter 37

# A Life Changing Prayer

I WILL TELL YOU now of an instance of praying that was intense and brought about a decision that affected our lives for years. When Dad was stationed in Trinidad for his first station after six weeks of training we found a church and were happy there. However we were across the state from our families and as you boys got older and were starting school we felt we needed to be closer to your grandparents, aunts and uncles as you grew up. We also found it hard to make ends meet as expenses were high there and the state didn't pay well then. As we thought about moving an opening for a patrolman came up in Leadville. We had moved from Leadville to Trinidad so knew what it would mean to go back. The altitude and harsh winters didn't agree with our health so it was quite a decision to make. We talked about it for several days and the word Leadville never left my mind.

One evening as I was washing up after supper I said a short prayer. Lord please tell us what you would have us do and where we should go. As I said, the name of the town was always on my mind as we mulled over this move.

The next morning when I woke up my mind was unable to think of Leadville. It was completely gone and never came back. I deliberately tried to think about that town, I could not think of its name. When I told Dad we knew we weren't supposed to move back there. So we waited to hear when and where or if we were to move. Dad put in an application for a transfer to any where in the northwest quarter of the state.

A few months later an opening came up in Kremmling. The patrolman stationed there was killed in an accident. Dad was offered that position. We asked God if this was the move to make and both of us got a mental yes. Dad had a week to move and be on duty in Kremmling which seems to be the way it goes when the Lord says go. We had to hurry a lot to make the move in time for him to start his job there. At first nothing seemed to work out as we couldn't find a house to rent but finally everything came together and we lived there thirty nine years.

Thirty some years later Dad's health started to get worse and the winters were becoming impossible to deal with. We started praying about it but never got the word we were to move to a lower climate. Thirty nine years it took for God to say go! So we started the process of moving. Everything fell into place so fast at one point I asked Him if we could slow down a little as I couldn't get everything packed that fast! I was serious about it.

We finally found a house we like and signed the contract in about twenty minutes. The move took some days but everything fell into place. We were sent to a church where we found a church family to replace the one we had left in the move and missed so much. So when you pray about something, be ready to get the word to do what He wants you to do. And hang on as sometimes it happens really fast.

# Chapter 38

## The Holy Spirit

In the gospel of John we are told how Jesus informed his apostles that He would be leaving them in a short while and why this had to happen. I paraphrase here, if I don't go away from you the Holy Spirit can't come into your lives and into this world. When I leave then the Holy Spirit will come and He will be your comforter, counselor and teacher in the things you need to know. When He comes be thankful for the presence of the Spirit. I suggest you read this part of John as it explains a lot better than I can.

The book of the Acts of the Apostles starting in chapter 2 tells us how this all came about and what an exciting time it must have been. The apostles had chosen a replacement for Judas who had gone away from them. They voted Matthias, sometimes called Bartholomew, to join them. They were all gathered in a room when suddenly there was a strong wind from heaven and they were all visited by tongues of what appeared to be flames. The Holy Spirit had come to them as Jesus had told them it would. So they understood why Jesus had to leave them. But what a joyful, wonderful experience it was when the Holy Spirit came. Read the book! What a gift!

I have included the above verses to tell you clearly of how and when the Holy Spirit, the third member of the Holy Trinity, came to earth to be with us when Jesus ascended to heaven. He is our Counselor and Comforter. We are baptized by water into Christ's family and receive the Holy Spirit within us. We are also told that our bodies are the temple of the Holy Spirit.

This may hard to understand and even harder to try to explain but its true. I have experienced many times when the Spirit manifests Himself in something I was doing. It is not to be feared when the visit happens but rather is a blessing, an assurance that through the Spirit the Lord is with me. Through the Spirit we are sheltered all the time. We choose to walk away from that shelter at our own risk.

Now that I have completely confused you about the Holy Spirit I will tell you about an instance of actually feeling His presence. On the day of Pentecost our denomination holds a special service of anointing and praying for the Spirit to be among us. Several years ago as I knelt at the communion rail during special prayers I felt the back of my hair flip about as though a breeze had gone by or someone had moved it with their hand. I didn't think anything of it until I mentioned it to others who were kneeling beside me to see if they had felt that too. No one had and then I started looking around to see if doors or windows were open to allow a wind to come through. There was nothing open to the outside that could account for my hair being moved. No one had been behind me to flip it either. I think others may have felt it too but they were too nervous to mention it for fear of being thought weird. Being thought weird doesn't bother me I guess.

When I talked to the priest about it he said the Spirit was playful at times and perhaps just wanted me to know He was around. I was in a struggle with my faith at that time and may have needed that assurance.

I truly believe everyone can know the presence of the Spirit if they will just open their minds and hearts to see what is happening around them.

I wrote this chapter some time ago so this is a past experience I tell you about now. I had an appointment to have a procedure done in the hospital on a certain date which was in conflict with something else that had come up. I had fumed and fussed around for about thirty minutes because I would miss the other thing I wanted to do. Not being prone to cancelling a doctor's appointment on a whim I made up my mind to do what had to be done and go to the doctor. As I made that decision the phone rang. The doctor's office called to cancel the procedure as it wasn't allowed to be done until a month later due to my heart problems. I had suffered a heart attack eleven months earlier and no procedures were to be done for at least a year. Also the procedure required that my heart medicines be stopped for a week prior to this procedure and that hadn't been done. I will never know what might have happened had the procedure been done just then. Maybe nothing serious, maybe something bad. Was I kept safe by spiritual intervention. I don't know. I just tell you about things that happen that are out of the ordinary.

Trying to tell you about the Holy Spirit if you haven't experienced His presence is nigh onto impossible for me. During the latter half of the twentieth century the Spirit began to be forgotten by people to the point that if we mentioned dealing with the Holy Spirit we were considered a little strange by some. Or some would just lightly speak of Holy Spirit without meaning a part of the Trinity and necessary to a healthy spiritual life.

As on the day of Pentecost when the Spirit first visited the apostles, we too have to experience Him. We can't see the Spirit but we can see His handiwork or feel His working within us at times we so badly need the gifts He gives us. Perhaps the reason people don't like to talk about the Spirit is that in years past the term Holy Ghost was used and anything that sounded spooky turned people away.

I can only tell you how I have been blessed many times by the Spirit being with me when I pray with others for healing of any kind and sensations of electricity or other manifestations happen. When I am in distress and praying hard for answers to problems I hear what He wants me to do or say or be. When I say hear I don't mean a physical voice but rather a quiet voice inside a space where nothing else can enter. Until He has given me the message I cannot free myself, the Spirit has taken over and only when He has finished am I able to go back to what I was doing. I am not talking about messages that are weird and asking me to do strange things, or things that would harm someone. The words are always simple, quietly said and make me comfortable most times and some times not so comfortable if I am told to change something I am doing. The words that are given may clear up a question I might have or give directions to take on some thing that will help others but always within my belief that the Lord won't ask me to do anything that would cause harm.

In another place I told you of the gifts of the Spirit. So now here are the fruits of the Spirit. In Galatians, we learn that there also fruits of the Spirit along with the gifts. Kindness, gentleness, patience, love, peace, joy, faithfulness and self-control.

I have put this in to assure you that the Holy Spirit is with us today, doing what He was sent to do. I have talked to some people about these gifts and they can't believe they happen. Some are of the mind, if I don't have one no one else can have one either. Some have asked for one or the other and been given it, others have asked and not been given. I don't know why except as it says above, it is up to the Spirit to make the determination. I won't try to tell you how that works out. I don't have a clue. That is one of those spiritual mysteries we can't grasp. Many have tried to define the Holy Spirit and have not succeeded, so how can I think I am able to do this. All I can do is witness the power and love I have experienced by allowing Him to lead me, teach me and sometimes boss me around. Once again I would say many have had their own time with the Spirit. Some won't talk about it but many will if given the opportunity. If they want to share with you, take time to listen. You will hear some great stuff.

So that is what I know about the Holy Spirit. I know

that when I pray for other people for healing of whatever else their needs might be the Holy Spirit comes to help me pray. I just let Him do the praying when this happens and sometimes we pray in a prayer language that no one understands. I am sure the Lord knows what it is I pray for as the prayer language was given to me by Him.

There are those folks who pray with others for healing or whatever their needs might be. I talked about this type of prayer earlier and explained that I am one of those who pray for others for healing.

I want to tell you about the experience of being slain in the Spirit or I prefer resting in the Spirit. This happens when the Holy Spirit comes, usually by invitation, into the scene. As the person doing the praying may in some small way touch the person being prayed for, that person may fall or drop to the floor. This can happen without those doing the praying touching the person they pray for. This is the Spirit taking over, is not bad but a blessing, and that person is not hurt by falling

I have been prayed for in such a way, being touched by one finger on the forehead or hand, and falling into a still state while remaining awake to what is happening around me. Once I cried for a long time, at other times I just feel refreshed and energized when I get up. I have seen some who put their entire hand on a person's head and start pushing them backward until they have to fall over. I have had this happen to me and I finally fall to keep from being hurt in some way. These people are not praying in the Spirit but using their own power to make it seem the Spirit is with them. They make me afraid for the people for whom they pray. When most of those who pray for others for healing merely lightly touch a person, the Spirit takes over, not always causing people to fall. Rather the quiet resting happens as they remain standing. This is a wonderful blessing to have happen to you and should not be shunned out of fear or disbelief. Just beware of the false teachers who may be innocent of their lack because of being trained by someone who was also a false teacher.

In the book of Joel a prophet, we are told that God will pour out the spirit on all people so the young will have visions and the old will have dreams and the young will prophesy.

This is hard to understand and even harder to try to explain but it is true. I have experienced many times when the Spirit manifests Himself in something I am doing. It is not to be feared when the visit happens. It's a blessing, an assurance that through the Spirit that the Lord is with me.

I suppose all the miracles I have told of in another chapter have happened with the Holy Spirit being involved, acting as God and Jesus' spiritual presence with us. Great thinkers and theologians wrestle with the definition of the Spirit and the role He plays.

They certainly have problems with it and I can't make a definitive statement about Him. I only know what happens when I pray and the Spirit answers my prayer or acts to save me. That is one of the beauties of our faith, the great mystery for which we have no answer—just reassurances that we are in the Lord's company.

There is a tremendous sense of God's power when He

gives us strength through the Spirit to endure suffering and grief, possibly more than when He heals a person. Not everyone is healed physically although we pray, plead, promise or bargain. He knows each of our needs much better than we do. What we see as physical needs may be more connected to emotional or spiritual conditions that need tending to. As I have prayed with others over the years it became apparent that the lack of trust in God, the unwillingness to bend our will to His can be a part of the illness or distress. This was true in my own healing when I finally gave over all control. I have spoken elsewhere about God not sending us sickness, pain, grief, stress or other problems that assail us. He is a loving God who would like His creation to be perfect and happy. We cause enough misery for ourselves and others. He doesn't need to add anything more. We are our own worst problems. As we were created with free will we use it willingly and much to our disadvantage, not thinking of short or long consequences but just what we want right now. We merrily go along with no thought of God or Jesus until something awful happens. Then we say why—how—did God do this to us. On the other hand if something good happens we say, aren't we lucky. Do you see my point.

When my sister Nina's one year old grandson developed a tumor behind his right ear she immediately wanted to know what had they done that God would do this to them. I told her if God wanted to punish them for something they had done they would have the tumor behind their ears, not the baby's ear. I don't know if she believed me.

I truly believe everyone can know the presence of

the Spirit if they will just open their minds and hearts to see what is happening around them. Too many times we are prone to say about something unusual, that is just a coincidence. Albert Einstein said, *a coincidence is God's way of remaining anonymous.*

Further reading of the Bible will tell you the prince Jesus talks about is Satan, sometimes called the father of lies, or other names. Don't give him any space in your life but don't imagine he is behind every tree or bush either. He is devious, sly, and waiting for an opening to enter into your life and wreak havoc with you if you let him. As you get along with your life little temptations that you know aren't right will crop up unexpectedly and you have to consider where that temptation might be coming from. He is sneaky.

The first time we hear of the Holy Spirit of God is in Genesis 1: 1through 2. I am sure you have all heard how creation began. If not read the above Scriptures.This tells us God's Spirit was present in the beginning with God and Jesus, Son of God. The Spirit of God hovered over the waters. I just read that in an ancient writing the Spirit was said to flutter over the waters, like a dove. This was written long before Jesus' time.These three we call the Holy Trinity.

Science has all kinds of theories about the beginning of creation that they use to avoid admitting to a Higher Power. Not all in the scientific field are of this mind as some are devout believers in God. The more they discover the more proof they find that there is a creator. Until they can tell me what went bang as in their big bang theory I will continue to believe that God did it in whatever way He chose. Science cannot yet refute the law of physics that says matter cannot create itself from nothing. There is a big invention in use by scientists who tell us they have found the God particle. But where did the particle come from originally. They have material already at hand to use along with the machine they have made from materials on earth. Tell me what that particle came from originally and then we will talk!

In the book of Romans Paul tells us we can call God Abba, Father. Daddy is the more informal translation of the word Abba. This phrase caused me some problems when trying to understand God as the word father to me was the earthly man who donated sperm to my conception. If that sounds harsh it is because my father was a mean man who had no gentle side for me until a lot later in my life when it no longer mattered. Father meant a harsh, judging, punishing being so the God I thought of then was better to not have too close. We speak of that God as being transcendent, or far away from us. Since then I have learned to love the immanent God, the one who is very near at all times and readily accessible to me and you. This is possible mostly through the Spirit of God who Jesus sent to be with us when He ascended to the Father.

If that just confuses you I am doing the best I can to help you grasp what a wonderful mystery it all is. We are not meant to understand all of it. Remember the Adam and Eve story about eating the forbidden fruit so they could be like gods themselves. I don't know what to make of that except to say it tells us we think we can be God. Can't be done, wasn't meant to be done and be wary of those who say it can be done! That is an age-old heresy going around right now. If someone tries to tell you they can show you how to become Godlike, tell them to get their own dirt and prove it.

# Chapter 39

## Listening to the Holy Spirit

When we pray and are answered it is good to take time to "listen" to see if God speaks to us. You will know when He does. He doesn't always use words but rather gives your mind a jog to tell you this is what you should do, or gives you a feeling of peace and calmness so you know all is going to be in His hands, that He has heard you. Sometimes He will speak into your mind in a way that is not aloud but that still voice will leave no doubt as to who is talking to you. It is an extraordinary thing to have happen and you will never forget it. A few people have told me He roars at them in a loud voice. They also say they really pay attention! Fortunately my experiences that I tell about in other places have been very quiet, calm and of few words. Questions demand an answer of me if it takes all day or night. He wants an answer. He expects us to heed what He is saying. Now I don't know if it is God, Jesus or the Holy Spirit who talks to us as I have never asked for identification! You will know by the absolute sense of being in a sacred place with a special being when it happens. Everything else is shut out and the world is still for that time. Strangely though I am also awake and aware of what is around me but I can't pull away and the outside noise stops. Whichever one it is doesn't waste a lot of words either but gets right to the point.

The last time it happened to me was when I was distressed about something going on in the Church Universal, meaning the world wide Christian church. As I questioned and prayed, prayed and questioned I was suddenly in a state of calm, quiet awareness. Then the still, small voice asked me if I was willing to die for my faith. Well I didn't breathe for a while then tried to go back to watching TV I could see to one side.

I didn't want to deal with that question the first thoughts being of lions, martyrs, gladiators and death. I was in that place of calmness for probably fifteen or twenty minutes, trying to come to an honest answer within myself. Finally I could with all honesty and faith answer yes. Then I was able to return to watching TV but didn't really care to. I had some serious thinking to do.

After a long time of meditating on what I had committed myself to I knew that I had answered truthfully. I think I added a little rider of please don't let it be too painful when it comes.

Throughout this I have told you of my encounters with the Lord or the Holy Spirit or God. I have never been able to separate the three and don't think anyone else can either. How can I tell who it is speaking to me, or holding me up when in grief, or sitting with me when I am in pain.

Not one of them has ever said this is God speaking, or I am Jesus or I am the Holy Spirit. Surprisingly the voice always sounds the same, the presence is always the same so I just go along and don't ask questions as to identity. I have learned over many instances that it is not a human voice that I hear or a human presence that comes near me to comfort and console me. Rather it is a spiritual voice and I daresay that as this is what this book is about. The spiritual that resides within us and with us is from God. I am sure you know well about the physical world that we live in. You have been tested, retested and tried again and again. I hope and pray you can discern the difference between physical and spiritual. When you aren't familiar with being in the company of one of the Holy Trinity it may be hard for you to figure it out. Don't be discouraged. Ask Jesus to help you and wait patiently until the answer comes.

## Chapter 40

# A New Way to Know God's Will

THIS IS A CHAPTER that will cause you to wonder if I have lost my mind or have become a zealot or whatever name people put on us who have had the blessings of seeing a vision or having dreams in which God teaches us something He would have us know. I assure you I am totally sane. You know me well enough to know I am not given to making up stories or taking anything as truth until proven so. I have had several dreams and had a few visions or other manifestations of the presence of the Lord, probably through the Holy Spirit. You have read earlier about how this comes about.

When I talk about God things such as hearing the still small voice speak to me, I assume it is the Holy Spirit acting as the voice of the Lord. Another thing I have learned to do is check out all events against Scripture and if it doesn't fit I don't accept it as valid. It might be the action of the father of lies, Satan, the devil, evil one, whatever name you call it.

Jesus refers to him as the prince of this world in the gospel of John 16: 11. Satan can place ideas in our minds that seem reasonable at the time but are going to cause us or someone harm in the end. Don't go looking behind every action or person as a doer of evil however. Sometimes, we in our innocence of God's wishes for us and Satan's presence in the world, do dumb things and wonder why later. You read earlier how St. Paul was confused as to why he would do what he knew he wasn't to do and neglected doing what he should be doing. Reread Romans: Chapter 7: 14 through 25 if you need to understand what I am talking about. He always tried hard to follow God's rules after he became a God follower rather than a persecutor of those who were God's people, but even with his special knowledge and empowerment by God he messed up. If Satan could mislead Paul we are probably more apt to wander around wondering why we have done what we just did. Now you know.

Back to the visions and dreams.

I don't hold myself to be special in God's plan or love except being as all of us are as His children. I am open to hearing his voice, seeing His presence in whatever way He shows me and listening to any instructions He gives me. It took me a long time to get where I could recognize these occurrences as coming from the Lord. They are outside my mind's ability to think up or create so I know from whence they come. Read them and know what I tell you is true. Believing it will help you in situations in your life as they have helped me in making decisions for many years. You may be able to see some things that have happened and recognize them for what they are if you admit that the Lord does talk to us. Some times He speaks in a quiet voice, other times he puts an idea into our thoughts that makes us wonder what is happening. This is especially true if it is outside of what we would normally think about. Some times He speaks to us in dreams and a few see visions. There are many ways He can choose to tell us what He wants us to do and it is up to us to recognize that it is the Lord directing us. I look back at times and wonder if maybe I missed the message. Can you relate to this.

The first vision happened after we had moved to Kremmling where our place of worship was a small chapel hardly big enough for two pews, an altar, an old pump organ and a little gas floor heater. You boys should remember those days. Services were held every Sunday with a visiting priest once a month celebrating the Eucharist and the rite of Morning Prayer other days. After a time we had a resident priest so the Eucharist was celebrated every Sunday. We spent a lot of time on our knees in those days and were expected to concentrate on the service of Eucharist and not be looking around or day dreaming.

For whatever reason one Sunday during the Prayer of Consecration I looked up and the entire southwest corner of the building seemed to fall away. As I looked I saw a vast number of beings bowing deeply on their knees around the altar and outside as far as I could see. I also dimly saw the mouth of the Gore Canyon, the mountains west of us and the fields between town and the mountains. The physical sights were dimmed but the beings kneeling were clear and of a slight rosy color. I didn't know what to do so I put my head down and went on in the service.

When I told my priest afterward we came to the conclusion this was a visit from the communion of saints which we call the faithful ones who have died. Since then I have learned this is referred to as being in a *thin place* that lets us see beyond our physical world. Many folks have this experience and know that when we read in the Bible about seeing through a dark mirror now and some day seeing more clearly we have been privileged to see more clearly for a short time.

At that time the Holy Ghost or Spirit was not acknowledged very much so wasn't even considered. Certainly angels weren't even in the conversation. Who believed angels really visited us here on earth. Only years later when I started hearing people talk about seeing angels did I realize those kneeling around the altar were angels of the Lord and how they bowed in deep reverence to the bread and wine that we take as the spiritual body and blood of Jesus in this service. We are told humans were created a little lower than the angels. Some ancient teachings say that the angels envy us because of our relationship with Jesus that they don't have. I can't trace that to the Scriptures but that doesn't mean it isn't in the Bible somewhere. That He died for our salvation is such a wonderful gift to us which they didn't receive they look at us with envy. I don't know if that is true but it sounds good! Since the vision I too revere that time of consecration and receive the bread and wine as holy and due the most reverence I have to give. Some faiths use bread and juice instead of wine which is fine as they are still partaking of and remembering the Lord's last supper.

Small children often can see angels when adults can't. A weekend at a spiritual retreat that included about fifteen hundred people is an instance of this. We adults studied in separate classes according to what we were interested in learning. The children had their own space in which to learn and play. After classes we would all gather in the big room that could accommodate this large group for a service of Communion. One of the children's teachers told me later that when they came into the room the four, five and six year old kids stopped, were looking up and exclaiming "Look at all the angels". Children could see them hovering over the group. We adults didn't notice a thing. Was being able to see the angels open to the children because their eyes had not yet been clouded by the world's trappings that seem to blind adults to God's presence. In their innocence they could see what we cannot easily see. In Scripture we are told that when the scales fall from our eyes we will be able to see clearly. Children's eyes may not yet have developed those scales of our world.

A very short special sighting, I would call it a vision, happened one summer day, bright sun and no rain falling on us. A half block down the street from our house I saw a gold shining veil that was hanging straight down over the street, not the houses just the street, from one side to the other. It didn't reach very high up into the sky. It was sheer enough to see through but solid enough to be seen easily. It was somewhat like the shoulder shawls women wear that are made to look like spun gold. There wasn't any thing holding it up nor any resemblance to a rainbow or that type of physical effect after rain as the day had been dry and warm.

It was only there for a few seconds and was gone. I questioned myself seeing this until I mentioned seeing it to a young boy, Jonathon, who lived up the street from us. He said he had seen the veil and wondered what it was. He described what he had seen in detail so I knew he had seen it too. Perhaps others saw it but I didn't go around the neighborhood asking questions. Folks may have thought me a little strange had I done that!

## CHAPTER 41

# Dreams Can Have Messages

IN SCRIPTURE WE ARE told that young men (and perhaps women) would see visions and old men would have dreams. I guess I fit in there between both as I was young when I had visions and older when I started having dreams that had meaning or instructions teaching me what I needed to know. Many people say they don't remember dreams and aren't sure they have dreams. I think every one has them but if not important they can't remember them. If you have dreams that seem not of the normal ones you have most nights, examine them to see if there is special meaning or teaching for you. Talk to someone who can explain dreams of this type. Be careful though as some folks think they can interpret dreams but put their own twist on them. They can cause you harm and problems. Remember I am talking to you as your mother and grandmother and would protect you from false teachers and fakes.

Dreams can be scary depending on what has happened in your life or what you have seen. I had many nightmares when young because I was allowed to see movies that we wouldn't let our little kids see today, or shouldn't anyway. *The Mummy, Frankenstein, The Werewolf,* etc. for a six to ten year old will impact her thinking for a long time. One result was a fear of the dark where all kinds of bad things lived. It probably just enforced my fear of most things that I had developed.

There are good dreams that some say are our mind's way of storing the information we have gathered that day, like filing it away for future use. That may be so. Other dreams I have had were directly connected either to action I was to take or information I had to learn. I know if I remember the dream the next day it has something for me to look into. Other dreams are nice but not remembered even if they wake me. Most of the dreams I am going to tell about happened in the 1980's and early 90's.

Dad was working for the State Department of Highways. He was a certified blaster, specially trained and qualified to handle explosives. When big rocks fell on the roadway anywhere in the area he was the one who got to blow them up to be small enough to be removed by the heavy equipment.

Byers Canyon between Parshall and Hot Sulphur Springs on Highway 40 was always dumping big boulders on the road, especially during the spring thaws. Because of this the road became wider than it was when we moved to that area. One side of the road is the rock wall and the other side is a steep drop into the Colorado River. If there was a rock hanging that looked like it would fall, the highway crew would take it down before it fell on a car.

One section of some large rocks had been watched

for some years and it was decided it was time to bring at least part of it down for safety's sake. Knowing this was to be done on Friday seemed to trigger a vivid dream on Thursday night. When I woke and remembered it I was really frightened as it showed me that your dad would be either seriously hurt by a rock fall or killed in a fall off the mountain. The minute I woke I started praying for his safety but didn't say anything to him so as not to plant that idea in his mind. When he walked in from work Friday evening I just thought, *well that dream was nothing after all.*

The next day a huge rock, as big as a railroad box car, fell and blocked Highway 40 going to Steamboat Springs. As it was a weekend day only Dad and his foreman were going to take care of the blasting so I got to ride along to take pictures. That went well but as I sat in the vehicle watching from a distance a good sized rock seemed to be coming right at me. It sailed over the truck but I didn't have time to take a picture. I was too busy ducking.

On the way to the site dad had been in the back of the pickup, putting out cones to stop traffic a long way back from the blast area. As his foreman slowly started up again, Dad fell off the back of the truck and rolled but didn't get hurt, just shaken up a bit. As we were on our way home I remembered that dream and thought that fall was what it was about. I tried hard to ignore the dream but it seemed the harder I tried the more it stayed with me. I was anxious to be finished with that dream and what it meant.

The next Monday morning the decision was made to take down the rock in the canyon. We had a camera that took pictures in fast series so a friend and I went to take instant action pictures of the blast. We were a long way back from the site so we could only guess at what the crew was doing most of the time. We saw them on the hillside above the rock, loosening anything that may fall on Dad as he set the explosives. They worked hard at this to be sure he would be safe.

He climbed a twenty or thirty foot ladder after he had mixed the explosives. I think he called it a chem-pack of some kind and was standing on a small rock ledge to place the charge behind the big rock. As he moved, a rock later estimated at about three hundred pounds, slipped toward him. He had his right hand full of explosives so threw up his left hand to try to force the rock away from him which may have saved his life. The rock glanced off his left hand scratching his wrist watch and the side of his safety glasses but as his right hand was also up, the rock pinned his right arm against the big rock. That pushed the rock away from him enough so he wasn't knocked off the side of the mountain. He was stunned and couldn't get down the ladder. Some of the crew had to climb up to him and bring him down.

He had placed the explosives after being hit and set them off when he was back on the road. This was because he was the only one certified to do that. Then he came wandering up the road to where I was taking the pictures. I only saw he was hurt when the rag he was holding to his head had blood on it. I took him straight to the hospital against his wishes where they found a concussion and also a damaged right elbow which later was determined to cause him thirty percent loss of use of that arm.

After all the excitement died down I remembered the dream. I learned from that to not ignore dreams that were meaningful in some way. I forgot to mention that my friend and I were praying for the crew while they were working on this job. God heard our prayers and kept Dad from being killed. He said later he knew he had to get the explosives placed. If not, if he fell off the ledge, the fall or the explosives would kill him if he was still holding them when he hit the ground.

These stories of my dreams aren't in the order they happened. I have kept writing journals for many years and keep noting these things but haven't put dates on them. My thing with dates I guess feeling they aren't that important.

In one dream I had died and was lying in a white satin casket and dressed all in white. Everything around me was white. White in dreams symbolizes purity or cleanliness. I had at this time made a serious commitment to become closer to the Lord and to let Him help me through life. As I was lying there in the casket my family, siblings and friends came by weeping and carrying on. I was trying to talk to them and tell them I was still alive. This was impossible to do and they continued to grieve until I woke up from the dream in great frustration at not being able to be heard. I didn't have a clue what this dream meant. Years later I told my priest about it. She said it may have meant that I had changed in my relationship with the Lord but was still myself. She thought it may have been involved with fear that my family wouldn't know me as I had changed somewhat, or that they wouldn't hear me tell them about the Lord, which was close to the truth. I wanted to share with everyone the peace and special relationship with the Lord that I had finally found. In the dream I became very frustrated with them because they couldn't hear me but thought I was dead to them. Who knows what all it meant.

Another dream similar to this occurred years ago. I was scheduled to have a face lift which for me was a real stretch as I would never consider that. I have had too many surgeries to have any elective surgery. This dream seemed so completely off the wall that for a long time I didn't try to figure out what it meant. I was seated in a doctor's office in the dark for a time. A doctor came in and started making marks on my face where he would do the cutting. Then he told me I would have to follow him to the roof, which didn't seem too odd to me. As I climbed a ladder he was behind me and started pulling on my feet. As he did this my skin seemed to fall away and by the time I got to the roof I was little more than a skeleton with a big gash across my skull where he had marked it. I wasn't frightened or worried as it seemed I was watching from a distance as all this took place.

When I finally decided to decipher this dream one day it came to me that this was a follow-up to the dream of being in the casket. The surgeon was Jesus and He had stripped away all of the old me so I could become a new person, fully cleansed with all sins and mistakes ripped away. I didn't know this but I was in the process of becoming the person He would have me be, trusting Him in all things and in all places.

In another dream I was walking through a pretty meadow on a country gravel road when I passed along a long row of hay bales neatly lined up. There were letters written on them in fiery flames which read, God reveals Himself in different ways to different people. Does this mean God reaches out to each of us in ways we can understand and hear clearly.

Some years later in a spiritual weekend retreat a man found the stone we had placed on his pillow that said "first stone". This is the lesson Jesus taught when a woman caught in adultery was brought before Him for judgment so the men could stone her. When he questioned her accusers as to who was so pure they could cast the first stone they all turned and went away. He did add that her sins were forgiven, to go and sin no more.

As we got ready to finish the classes in the retreat closure this young man said he now fully understood that he wasn't to judge others as he had been doing all his life. Rather he was to look inside himself and find what was keeping him from a full relationship with God. God revealed Himself to this fellow through a stone. This was not in my dream, but the dream revealed to me that God does teach all of us in a way we can understand and the young man's experience affirmed the dream.

In one dream your dad and I were walking, again through a nice meadow, just visiting and enjoying the scenery. As we went along the way we saw a large pipe, probably like a water main but not big enough to walk into. I heard a voice say, you stay where you are and I will communicate with you. You will be a pipeline of mine. The voice came through the pipe. We moved on a little ways and felt comfortable and good as if this was an every day occurrence. We had been pondering moving to another church but after this dream I shared with your dad we decided we were meant to stay put. Since then I have been called to a healing prayer ministry at this church that continues until I hear God tell me to stop.

The next dream happened within the last few years and fully caught my attention. Again everything was white and as I stood at the foot of a steep mountain I knew I was to climb it. Off in the far distance I could faintly see a small house on one side and a small group of houses that were very dim on the opposite side. Other than those there was nothing except a white something that I had to walk through to climb to the top. It looked like snow but when I picked some up it wasn't cold or wet and had a texture like nothing I knew. It was hard climbing, as I took a step my foot would sink down into it almost to my knees. I would struggle to raise one leg and take a step while rooted with the other one in this white stuff. I started questioning myself, wondering what I was doing and considering going back to the bottom a few times. Something made me keep climbing until I finally reached the top, muscles sore, worn out and breathless. As I looked around back to where I had came from all I could see was white. I turned and looked down the other side of the mountain into a beautiful green valley with a stream running through it, trees and grass growing everywhere and a very steep side of the mountain to go down if I decided to choose that way. Some would say this is the slippery slope we take that leads us into places we should not be. I seemed to know I had been brought here to make a choice. The green valley was the world, the white mountain was life with the Lord and I had to decide which one I would choose. I started back down side I had just climbed. Although the walking was still hard it didn't take long to get down that mountain. When I woke the next morning I tried to determine what the dream meant and what I was supposed to do.

It may have been brought about because of the unrest and upset in the Christian faith today. We are told by Jesus to love God with all our hearts, all our minds and all our souls and to love our neighbors as ourselves. In this time too many churches are turning more into social clubs that entertain their people rather than help them find and worship God. They are more interested in money and possessions than feeding the hungry, giving the needy a helping hand and especially making sure our children are safe and taken care of. Not just the nice children but all children, as they all are His children. If all you have to share is a kind word or a smile it doesn't cost anything but may help people know they have been seen and not looked past as if they are nonexistant. I wrote a poem about this several year ago called Compassion. It is in the poetry chapter.

I am still trying to work through this dream, as I am in conflict regarding how many churches today say they have the right message for people. Not one can say they have heard from the Lord that the Bible is no longer relevant and can be dismissed as unnecessary for us to live by. Rather we hear that God wants us all to 'don't worry, be happy' without letting Him into our lives. I refer you again to the book of James regarding this. And the leaders wonder why the people are leaving their congregations so rapidly. People want a relationship with the Lord that is real, not one made up that tells them they don't need Him in their lives. I haven't yet been told by the Lord that I am to move to another place, but if and when that message comes I will do as I have in the past, follow what He tells me to do.

After work one day we were on our way to Denver and had been travelling for about twenty minutes. This was while I was ill with scleroderma and was tired all the time. I started to drift into a light sleep when I dreamed that the car was going straight off the road instead of turning with the curve we were in. I woke up, heart racing, expecting to crash but found every thing was fine and Dad was driving on the road without any trouble. I didn't know what prompted that dream.

As tired as I was, I was wide awake and didn't feel the need for sleep anymore. We had our visit and were on the way home, me wide awake, as I have never been able to sleep in a car since then. We had just crossed the Colorado River bridge headed north just outside town. I saw we were going straight instead of turning into the gentle curve we were in. I looked at Dad and he had dozed off. I quietly called to him so he wouldn't overreact and turn the wheel too far. He wasn't completely asleep, had just dozed off so it wasn't hard to get his attention. If he hadn't roused up and turned we would have gone straight off the road down a steep bank into what is a marsh or swamp.

In my dream I had seen the car going end over end. Had we gone off the road now we would probably have done just that as it would have been straight at sixty miles an hour. I believe that sometimes we do get a warning of trouble ahead and that has happened to me by dreams. Some folks have had other ways of being warned. I have to wonder how many times we are given a heads- up and didn't know what it meant or just ignored it

I have had many dreams since dad died and all have been comforting and usually included doing fun things. We have gone on boat rides, picnics and just enjoyed whatever we were doing. Never have I had a sad dream about him which is such a blessing.

I will tell you one that was a little different. My daughter in law Lisa and I were at a carnival or circus in line buying tickets. We were having trouble with the ticket seller for some reason and in frustration I looked away to my left. There was a group of people standing in what looked like a shallow boat and Dad was there too. I knew it was him because he had on the tacky brown fall coat he wore until it was almost in rags. He really liked that coat. He looked at me, he looked wonderfully calm and happy and it seemed he was calling me to come join him. Somehow I knew I couldn't do that. After a short time the boat started to move away down the stream and went out of sight. It made me feel okay and to understand that he had moved on into the next phase of our eternal life. I was comforted knowing he was taken care of and going where he should be. That is the only dream with him that wasn't full of fun and laughing and enjoying wherever we were. I haven't had many dreams with him in them since then.

As I look back over my journals of dreams and visions

I know now how important they have been in directing my journey on the pathway I have chosen, the path to follow Jesus no matter what life hands me. It is much easier to get through bad times when I can tell Him about my problems, listen for any advice He may have or just turn it all over to Him to take care of.

In my early years I had a recurring dream that was dreadful. I was driving a car full of people, maybe family, in a city with narrow brick streets and tall brick buildings. I was trying to get away from a carload of people who were chasing us. In the first place the dream would have to be considered ridiculous as I would never be driving in a city which looked like that one, tall brick buildings and nothing but narrow brick streets. It was always the same though. In each dream I would drive so fast around corners and up hills that weren't in any way familiar. I would wake up so frightened. The dream repeated several times until when it started I would wake up before it became too involved. Only after I committed myself to follow the Lord did it stop. It took some time to realize I wasn't having that dream anymore. Was I being chased by Satan to keep me away from my commitment to the Lord. Or was I being pursued by the Lord to bring me out of my lifestyle of confusion and problems. I don't have a clue! I am sure it was one or the other.

The latest dream I have had came about because I was stumped for a title for this book. I had one name for it when I was writing it only for my family but it really doesn't fit now. Before I went to bed one evening I asked the Lord what He would like the book to be called. Only when I woke the next morning did I remember the dream I had of finding groups of flowers growing in black, rich soil. Either the Lord who was walking with me, or I dug them out and took them to the edge of a town where there was nothing but a few weeds growing and empty lots, only dry, hard soil. I watched as those flowers were planted in that place of arid soil. So that is how this book came to have its name.

I end this chapter on visions and dreams, knowing there will be people who are skeptical and will laugh and discount what I have said. That's okay with me as we all make decisions as to what to believe. Scary dreams can sometimes be a wake-up call that change is needed in your way of living. Wonderfully fun filled dreams may let you know that you are doing okay. Each of us should look closely at dreams we have to see what they might be saying to us. The Lord does speak to us in several ways and dreams are one of those ways.

# Epilogue

I have been reading the book *It Really is All About God* which has caused me to look carefully at what I believe, to where that belief has brought me, and if I want to stay in that belief. If you are complacent about your faith and feel you have all the right answers I suggest you read this book. I don't remember what paragraph or page I was reading that triggered the following thoughts but it stopped me cold until I had examined and wrote what I tell you now.

As I write my story I have the advantage that age brings. You all are still struggling with jobs you don't like that don't pay enough, are boring or whatever else makes your days dreary. Sicknesses visit you and your family with attendant fears and concerns. Decisions must be made and you don't feel equipped to make wise ones. All of this is part of life. I have been through all that. I know what fear for family is and still get concerned for all of you if anything is about to overwhelm you. I have had the excitement of good things happening, births of babies, celebrations for any reason. I no longer deal with most of those things. We speak of walking on a path with the Lord but even though you may not feel this is the case for yourself, you are walking the path of life you chose or which was chosen for you.

My pathway has been a journey with the Lord. It now is set firmly in place with an end in sight. Now don't get excited yet, thinking I am at death's door. I don't think I am but we can never be sure. I do try to not step out in front of moving vehicles or drive into solid items such as walls or the like. However I did drive off a slight embankment when trying to park at a restaurant one day. I don't like to think about that. Others like to rehash what they saw. In good humor of course. In analyzing the incident I think I was in reverse and the car was in drive. I did knock down a handicapped parking sign. I offered to pay for it but the restaurant owner said it was not necessary. On a later day he told me someone had stolen the sign. I guess everyone needs a portable handicapped parking sign they can use as needed.

I am better now taking care of my self than I have ever been. I don't relish having any more problems than I have now. However one of the surprises that aging brings is that our bodies tend to wear out no matter how well we treat them. A heart that is wearing out inside and out will probably be instrumental in my end here on earth. Or maybe not, who can tell. Doctors won't commit to a definite answer. They don't know.

I don't know and don't worry about it. My feet are now walking slowly and hobbling along towards that door that we all must go through. As the years have passed, slowly at times and rapidly at other times, I have managed to live life to my fullest ability. I do sit and think, *where did all the time go*. I don't sit around wishing I could do this or that. Great waster of time! Instead I go and do as I can and as

I please and enjoy every minute of it. That wisdom comes with aging too.

As the doorway becomes clearer to me it is with anticipation I see it. What is on the other side. I have always wanted to know more. Glimpses of God's presence have assured me it is a real place and I believe the promise made to us that it is different and better than here. Matthew 28: 20 tells us Jesus will be with us until the end of the age.

Not to worry my dears. I will have to wait for my life plan to work its way through without my help in ending it. I really don't want to explain to the Lord that His death on the cross can be taken so lightly by me that I can snuff out His gift of life to me so easily.

Each book I read, each prayer I pray, each visit with family and friends is boosting me along my path. I am having a good time most days just being here and being wherever and doing whatever my mind takes me to.

This may sound unfeeling or unloving but it isn't. When Dad died, for the first time in my life at age seventy two, I could make decisions about what to do or where to go without considering anyone else at that moment. That isn't as selfish as it sounds. My entire life was enmeshed with parents, siblings, husband and children who I loved and enjoyed so much.

I was living at home with my parents, working but not making enough for a place of my own, when Dad and I married. I moved into a new home with dad and then you boys came along so I was never able to think only of myself in what I decided to do at any time. I now can say aye or nay in a way that is freeing, albeit lonely at times. I guess it is some compensation for being alone. Who knows. Again, I don't worry and overwork my mind about it, I just do it. One side effect is that if I am wrong I cannot share the blame with anyone. Darn.

So I have come to the end of my story to you. I have written in truth all that you read. Some of the events caused me to question if I really wanted to share those but to make my story whole and help you learn from it I had to tell all. Doesn't that sound dramatic. Just know that I love you all with my whole being and want only the best for you. You all have given me much joy and pleasure by being part of my family and I thank you all for that. Believe me when I say I would never say anything that will harm you or lead you down a bad road. Enjoy life, really stop once in a while to not only smell the roses but the see the colors as they truly are, feel the sun as it warms your body, and don't be afraid to look under rocks. There is a whole world under some of them.

I added some pages with quotes, some heavy and some humorous, to help you see a little deeper into how interesting life can be with the Lord. I have favorite theologians, not many, and favorite authors who I quote to demonstrate a point.

I added an appendix of my poetry, written over decades. Some were given to me in almost complete form as I was doing something else, like watching TV or cooking. This happened often enough that I learned to keep pencil and paper handy so I could write as fast as possible to get the poem down right. I also learned not to try to understand what was coming until it was finished or I would have to write the last lines myself. This accounts for some of the odd endings. I don't understand how or why, just write as fast as I can. Hasn't happened in a while so I don't know if what is to be said is finished or not. I hope you like the poems and prose I include for you.

So my dears it is time to sign off and wish you good reading. All praise and glory to our Creator Father, our Savior Jesus and to Our Counselor and Comforter the Holy Spirit! Thank you for your love. Because of your presence, love and guidance I have become this person I am today.

## APPENDIX A

# Words of Wisdom

I HAVE LOOKED TO so many wise people's quotes during my life. They all seem to fit any situation when I most needed to hear their words of wisdom. I didn't want to insert them into my story so as not to disturb the line of thought. I am including them here as I hope they will give you insights as they have done for me.

One of my favorite authors is C. S. Lewis who is known as the lay person's theologian of the last century. He wrote so many books, essays and articles I have never found time to read all of his works. The books I have read are written on a level most folks can understand with a little bit of study and seeking. He was an atheist for many years but found the Lord at some time. He was quite surprised to discover the truth of God's presence in his life. His book *Surprised by Joy* is about that discovery.

In his book *Reflections on the Psalms* he makes several statements I like, probably because I agree with them. On page 109 he says, the real reason why I can accept as historical a story in which a miracle occurs is that I have never found any philosophical grounds for the universal negative proposition that miracles do not happen.

Many people have tried to deflate stories of miracles. I don't know why unless they are of the mind that if it hasn't happened to them it can't happen. Or maybe they have had a miracle and can't recognize it. I wish people were more open to seeing a miracle when it happens.

Lewis also says, Jesus preaches but does not lecture. Therefore his teaching cannot be grasped by intellect alone.

So many theologians have argued one case after another by intellectually approaching it. They never can come to a solid answer because Jesus, God, cannot be learned by mind, intellect or whatever you like to call it. He has to be experienced spiritually to truly find Him as He is. This doesn't happen by reading about Him. Reading will open your mind to further discovery and will whet your appetite for a closer look to see the truth of His presence. He is waiting for you to begin that journey and will be most happy to come to you, to walk with you as you explore life with Him.

In the same book Lewis says, On three levels we meet the same refusal of what we might have thought best for us. 1 in the Word Himself, 2 in the apostle Paul of the Gentiles, 3 Scripture as a whole. Since this is what God has done, we must conclude, is best. It may be that what we should have liked would have been fatal to us if granted.

This is to me the best explanation as to why our prayers are not answered sometimes as we prayed them. We trust

God to always give us what is best for us, not just what we think we need. We cannot see the future and what we ask for might bring harm to us. He knows, so to protect us He chooses to give what is in our best interest. This is doesn't set well with us because our needs are opposed to our wants.

In another section of the same book Lewis gives us the idea of God's way as opposed to ours. He says, The conjectures we have as to why God does what He does are probably of no more value than my dog's idea of what I am up to when I sit and read.

This is a good explanation of our not knowing what God is doing or why. Does your pet know what it is you do or why you do it. Put yourself in the place of the pet, you sitting at God's feet trying to figure out what His infinite mind is thinking.

On people having free will Lewis says, There are two kinds of people. Those who say to God, Thy will be done. And those to whom God says, thy will be done.

On more than one occasion I tried to tell God what He should do and He seemed to say to me, thy will be done. Much to my sorrow it didn't work out too well for me. When I finally learned to say Thy will be done to God, things went much more smoothly. He never led me into a bad place or caused me pain. Rather He was there to comfort, strengthen and lead me to where I was meant to be.

Some Bible quotes you might not know give us good advice when we take them to heart.

From the second book of Timothy, the time will come

when men will no longer want to hear the truth of the Lord but will gather around the them those who will teach what they long to hear, to please them in what they want to do.

In Isaiah we hear to not be afraid for He has redeemed us, He has called us by name so we belong to Him.

First Corinthians reminds us that were bought with a price so we are not our own. Jesus dying on the cross for us was the price paid.

Romans chapter 8 assures us that if God is for us who dares to be against us. After all He gave His own Son that we might have life eternal.

Isaiah chapter 55 reminds us that we don't have God's way of thinking or doing things, His ways are different than ours.

One of my favorite Psalms is 139. I would like you to read the entire Psalm as it is full of what God has done and is doing. It answers questions about some of the things I have written about and maybe even answer some of your questions. It is much too long to paraphrase and would lose much of its meaning to do so.

Most of the following quotes have been around so long no one is sure who gets credit for them.

- You must see in others more than they see in themselves if you are to help them.

- Fear is faith in Satan.

- We are as little as the things we let bother us.

- When you feel so alone, unloved and down, can you remember that Jesus is with you, if you invite Him in.

- The will of God for us is what remains of a situation after we try without stint and praying without ceasing to change it.

- Death has taken away your loved one. Jesus has taken your loved one away from death.

- Jesus was the unwanted sent into the unknown to do the unthinkable for the ungrateful.

- From the book, *The Cloud of Unknowing,* by love God can be caught and held, by intellect never. By a monk named John thought to have lived in medieval times

- When Carl Yung was asked if he believed in God, he replied, No I don't believe in Him, I know Him.

- From J. T. Kendall:
  Definition of Grace (God's Grace) *Getting what we don't deserve.*

Definition of Mercy (God's Mercy) *Not getting what we deserve.*

- From my thoughts: Enjoy whatever stage of life you are in. You won't get a chance to repeat it even if you would like to.

- When you cherry pick the Bible (choose just the verses with which you agree) you get a very stilted image of who God, Jesus and the Holy Spirit really are. You also do not understand what God would have us be.

- If we were all asked to place the cross we carry (our burdens) in a room, we would take ours to the door and slip our cross quietly into the room. Then we would be asked to go into the room and take a cross that better suited us. When we saw the huge crosses others had placed, letting us see what others have to carry, we would quietly pick up our own smaller cross and walk away.

# Appendix B

# *My Poetry*

## A TIME TO LOOK BACKWARD

*Mona Blandford 2001*

If I could but walk this path again
I would stop and look at everyone and thing closely,
I would say in truth what they meant to me
And hold them in my heart gladly.

I would worry less about what people thought
And try to please God more,
I would recognize my own true worth
And not run away as I have before,

From closer relationships with those I love,
Let down the walls that ban them
To come too close and let them in
If hurt came in with them—I would manage.

To know early on that I was God's child
And be comfortable in that place,
To fear no thing that could occur unless
My soul was in danger grave.

To know the victimhood of mine
Was put upon me by others,
That I don't have to carry that cross
That I was not to blame.

To accept responsibility for what I have done
And confess it, accept forgiveness,
go on, letting it go into the heart of Christ
No longer mine to carry, unloaded and at last set free.

But I'm afraid that cannot be so
As I look back again.
As I walk on this long, long path
That slowly will someday end,
I hope and pray those who remember me
Will not say I'm glad she's gone
To accept the facts as they are true
To know I have made a difference
To hope those I love and loved knew,
Before they were taken by death that I loved them.

## FAITH

*Mona Blandford 1996*

This morning I am looking out toward the mountains.
It is cold and damp and a heavy gray
cloud hangs over them.
I know those mountains are there with their peaks,
Snow capped and rocky, with pine trees.
Yet I cannot see them with my eyes.
Today my faith and belief in God is stronger because
Although I cannot see Him, I know
He's there behind those clouds
He's holding my hand, holding me up, keeping me strong.
I have many heavy clouds in my life. Some have
lifted to reveal the truth behind them
Some still remain and only God
knows the truth behind them.
I am grateful for this cloud, this cold, because is
has shown me an important part of who I
am and how strong my faith is.
Faith is knowing the mountains are behind the clouds,
Faith is knowing that the Lord is walking
with me although I cannot see Him.

## A HYMN OF PRAISE

*Mona Blandford 1988*

To the Father, Son and Holy Spirit, blessed
Triune Godhead, Creator, Redeemer and
Comforter.
In joyful thanksgiving for all we have received.
We give you praise and glory.

We lift our lives to you in humble love
We offer you our weaknesses and our strengths
To be used as you would direct us.
We offer to you all that we are that we may be
purified and sanctified by your grace.

Holy Father, we see your creation and glorify your name,
We experience you gift of steadfast love
and in awe we give you thanks.
The wonder of your gift of Your Son
astounds us and we give you thanks.
We proclaim your wonders to all the
world and we give you thanks.

Blessed Son, we honor and praise and exalt
your name before all those around us.
We approach the Father through your life, oh
Holy One and we give you thanks for the
gift of your redeeming sacrifice.
You, our Savior our teacher, the wonderful gift
from God, we praise you and glorify you
forever.

Holy Comforter, stay with us now.
Gift from God and Son, we thank you
for your presence in our lives.
Be by our side in all the world, our help in daily living.
Let your fire burn within us always,
in our hearts and minds.
We give thanks for your wonderful
presence within and around us.

Love hope salvation begins and ends in
You, Father, Son and Holy Spirit.
Hallelujah!

## JUDGMENT VERSUS COMPASSION

*Mona Blandford 1988*

As I meet all the people with heavy, furrowed brows,
Their constant expressions are dark, gloomy scowls,
How can I know what pain they now feel.
Or what sadness a forbidding look helps to conceal,
Are their souls, to God, less precious than mine.

The desperate look of those alone and so lonely.
Whose youth is now gone, well spent but gone, only
To live with their feelings not being needed,
By old age and sorrow being defeated.

The young ones so urgently searching for ways
To cope with their problems day after day.
In a world of indifference that has gone far astray
Yet beckons them follow through a self serving maze.

The dirty, the ragged, hungry, sick ones and poor
Whose lives are so hard they can struggle no more
They barely exist in a world they can't fathom,
A world that rejects them as ugly and loathsome.

As I bow my head and swear love of the Lord,
How I pray He will help me to follow His word.
Help me to see more the soul, less the shell,
Hear the song that it sings, see not the state of the bell.
Help me to see Him in all the people I find
Remembering their souls, to God,
are as precious as mine.

## MEDITATIONS

*Mona Blandford 1998*

Lord I come now to ask for help
I lay before you the questions on my heart,
Only by sharing them with you can
I reach a state of peace.
Even if no answers are forthcoming,
I cannot carry their pain alone
What more can I do to affect a change
in the world around me.

Prayers are constantly offered and
actions are taken by me,
But my efforts seem so trivial and
aren't very change-causing.

The world is in trouble—the human
condition is deteriorating into
something very ugly in many places.

The greatest obscenity ever was your death
upon the cross. Today people mock and
abase your death and call it art. Foul words
that denigrate the human condition and
advocate violence against people,
especially women, is called music.

Freedom of speech is held as a beacon but
tramples on freedom from ugly
harassment by verbal garbage.

Freedom of choice is held as a right and the
ensuing responsibility for actions is
ignored or called too harmful.

Good and uplifting teachings and thoughts
are jeered at as being soft or sentimental.

Lord, how much easier it is to stay in your
presence and meditate and bask in your love.
It is hard to risk telling of your love to others.
My Mary side is so comfortable. My
Martha side knows that now only is cleaning
and washing necessary—but any work
on your behalf is to be done. Telling and sharing—
bringing and taking for those who are
in need.

Mary is passive—Martha is active.
Which is easier for me to be today

# PEACE

*Mona Blandford 1988*

When I give Him my anger He gives my calm
When I give Him my fears He gives me courage to follow Him

Giving Him my sins Brings His forgiveness
My anxiety Becomes a peaceful trust
My pain delivered becomes Spiritual healing
When I suffer lack of direction He gives me dreams to follow
He turns my tears of sorrow Into tears of joy
When I gave Him my life He gave me eternal life in His Grace

And Peace

Washed away are the webs that once
bound the corners of my soul,
No longer does the ache of loss and hurt
pull me into the darkness of despair
A calm trust has quieted the fear that once controlled me.
Within the very deepness of my soul dwells
the burning presence of His Holy Spirit
Which causes me to stand in awe of His glory.
I have become a freer person than I once was
by being always in His wonder filled
Presence.
I am more rather than less
He has freed me to follow Him.

## REMBERANCES

*Mona Blandford 2007*

There is a pain within me
So deep I seldom touch it now
Enclosed in a wall I have built around
It stays forbidden to surface unless
I allow it so.

The leaves, gone from green to gold,
Soon year four without him will begin,
Surprise to myself, I have made it this far
Another anniversary brings not joy
But some peace.

## UNTITLED

*Mona Blandford 2009*

Don't sing to me your silvr'y songs of
fame and power or earthly things,
I care not for gold nor gems nor foolish human triflings.
Tell me of the created world-of beast
and flowers and birds awing,
That praises raise with nature's
gifts—unto our risen King.

The glory of the sweet smelling flowers,
the majesty of ancient trees
The joy we find in a small child's smile
or the droning of the bees,
Winds that blow a freezing snow in
winter holds life inert in cold
Then life renews itself each spring
as it has since time untold.

A gentle stir of aspen leaves speaks of
secrets my eyes cannot behold,
The whisper of a baby's breath tells of
a mystery that life itself enfolds
As we look with wonder at the Pole Star in a midnight sky
Or see a moth beat at a flame only to
die, we ask ourselves, why.
How quickly slips our hold on life,
The leash that holds us all together,
The body falls, a soul ascends,

A blink of an eye, a breath exhaled
So another life comes to its end.

Perhaps if we could see the hand that
fast comes near to call us
Would we walk away from the false
gods for which we have lived,
Would we be filled with love and joy of family and friends
Or still close our eyes to that on which our soul depends.

## SLOWLY WITH DIGNITY

*Mona Blandford 1982*

Her pace is very slow, measured and cautious
The gray, musty rustle of age whispers
as a shadow at her heel.
Her feet are set upon a harder path
than we will care to follow
But follow her in years to come, we will.
As children, we leaned on shoulders now
stooped with age and sorrow
Her hands so twisted and painful now, once dried our tears,
How sad, the metamorphosis of a soft and loving nature
Brought to a hard, dour stridency, by grief and many years.
Each path we've walked in life, she walked before us.
She too was young, had loves, dreams and fears,
As though to clear a path, she walked for us to follow
But could not spare us, though she
would, our fair share of tears.
She laughed with us in times when we were happy,
Exulted for us when we exceeded our wildest dreams
She suffered along with us in pain and tribulations,
And was always there to help by any means.
Now the time of quiet preparation is upon her
As she bit by bit retreats into her land of memories
And though she's treading upon unknown pathways
She's showing us how to walk slowly, but with dignity.

I wrote this poem for my mother as she slowly
became more dependent on others

## THE BOX

*Mona Blandford 1988*

Four walls and top, the box wherein I live
Has closed me in, of myself I no longer give.
By self-serving ways so tightly wrapped
By lack of love of others I stand entrapped.

If I look back to try to see where I fell off
The road of life and chose this narrow trough,
Where I deal with folks no more, only my life
I care not for others or about their strife.

I see two paths, one hard with pain
Always surrounded by personal gain,
The other one of softer ways
Of love and kindness and happy days.

Both paths seem to run for an equal time
Side by side, they reflect this life of mine.
Offsetting the pain and worry and sorrow
Are the joys of love and new tomorrows.

It is plain at last that my trials are not worse
Than most who have stayed on the course,
Who haven't pulled away to hide their eyes
From sights to painful to see, they were wise
Enough to know life is hard, it is true,
But it is only a brief time of passing through.

If we would help others we meet along the way
And know their needs go on day after day,
Then our own cares and worries most certainly would
Become easier to bear, the box of self care should
Slowly break down from lack of tending,
By our constant serving of others unending,
Then the paths of pain would be more easily trod
And the path of joy would be a journey with God.

## THE CHOICES WE MAKE

*Mona Blandford 1989*

I set my feet upon a pathway
To walk straightway to the end,
But many a detour and side trip I've taken
Circled around, got lost and then came back again.

This path I travel at times goes through
Beautiful gardens and green places to rest my eyes
Then the Lord walks beside me
And hears the praises my grateful heart does cry.

But other times the path roams and wanders
Through hot and sand swept plain
Where only thorns and cactus grow,
And biting winds drive sand into my face.
And then I feel the Lords hand reach out
To lead me through the troubled times
As I take His hand I am again sheltered by His grace.

No thing this world can throw at me
Can harm more than body or mind,
My soul, the who I really am,
Is safely tucked behind the Shield
Of His protection—that wraps me round about
His love and sacrifice holds true and closes evil out.

He is my Savior, Redeemer and lover of my soul.
He died to keep me whole!
Thank you Lord!!

## THE POTTER AND THE CLAY

*Jeremiah 18*

*Mona Blandford 2008*

On the potter's wheel I was cast
Unshaped, unknown, unnamed
Except to God.
The gentle hands began my forming
A quiet love held me close,
My spirit already blessed and known.

And then the world became my outside home
A world that could and would break me into pieces
A physical and mental breaking that left
Only an empty clay pot.

Spirit safe, God sheltered and protected
Nothing can go there without
His and my admittance
He is the rock that is unbroken,
That evil breaks itself against.

The potter reclaimed the clay,
That empty pot no longer useful,
And cast it on the wheel once more
Reshaped, renewed, re-created, a new beginning.

So no surprise for this creation this time
A stronger, strengthened clay was used,
One fired in the crucible of life,

A heated, intense creation that knows its Maker.
An assured and receiving one who
knows the voice of its Creator.

Hears and obeys, goes, does at His bidding
Listens with outer and inner ear,
Willing and able, eager,
Once broken—knows the road to travel.
To beware the wiles of the world.
With God's help, will not be cast again upon the wheel!

## COMPASSION

*Mona Blandford 1988*

The world as seen through a
Mother's eyes are
Oft times not too clear
She looks at her child in great surprise
when first the baby appears,
As years go by and the child grows up
the eyesight seems to dim,
She sees the person but her heart knows
there is more than that to him.

Mothers have the built in love that overlooks the wrongs
And sees the good, as a mother should,
and believes her child is strong
Enough to overcome the world and to
succeed in all that he essays.
Even the passing of years untold holds
a promise of better days.

Hope always lives in a mother's breast
that a child will find the way
To live and be happy in his life's choices
though both their heads are now gray.

So when you see a lost, lonely soul,
unkempt, unclean, poor, rich or ill,
Remember his mother loves and believes in
him and until her death always will.

Judge him not by his worldly state, you
know not what brought him here.
Look as if with a mother's eyes and see his soul still dear.
And know that God also loves him
as much as He loves you.
If his mother and God can love this child of theirs
Then why in the world can't you.

Don't pass by, no matter the state of
a soul who needs another
To recognize he's still alive and is
asking little of sister or brother
Just bless him friend with a word or two
and a helping hand in any guise,
Not all gifts are coin or food, a smile, if that
is all you have, will very nicely suffice.

# TIME

*Mona Blandford 1988*

"Come visit with me and take my hand"
So often I've heard Jesus say,
My ears were closed and I hoped He'd understand
As I replied, I just don't have time for you today.
The kids need bathed, I must make the bed
There's someone around who needs to be fed
Or there's a cobweb on the ceiling.
Yet I've called Him for help so many ways
I'm so glad He's never answered me with
"I just don't have time for you today."

## INVITATION

*Mona Blandford 1998*

I saw the Lord approaching
With hands held out to me
He said, come child, I love you
In my pride and pain I mumbled,
Not me, not me, not me.

I've done some really bad things
I'd rather He not see,
He said, come child, I love you,
I lowered my eyes and stammered,
Not me, not me, not me.

He said, my child I know you—
And share the pain you bear,
Come child, know that I love you
I looked into His loving eyes,
And said, maybe, maybe, maybe.

I stepped, faltered, stepped again
And reached for the hand of God
He said, come child, I love you
I felt His love wash over me and I answered
Yes me, Yes me, Yes me!

## HANDICAPPED

*Mona Blandford 1996*

The blinded one, though he cannot see,
Would know me far better than you know me.
His eyes can't see the false face shown
To the world to hide the fear of weakness, known
To bring the pleasure my enemies would find
In knowing that I am troubled in heart and mind.
For he hears the pain with which I am indwelt
And senses the agony that I have felt.
His ears hear words that remain unspoken
Words that whisper of a heart so broken.
It is I, who is handicapped because I only see
Until I can relate to others and their sorrow ascertain,
It would be better to seal my eyes and only hearing then
Be blessed to truly see clearly again.

## LAMENTATIONS

*Mona Blandford 1982*

I have walked the paths where pioneers once wandered,
I have breathed where only the strongest once survived,
Was it that their strength was more than mine is now,
Or only that their trials were more simplified.

I too stand firm on faith long held to guide me,
And have been bent by sorrow and life's pain
I have bowed my head, my back, my knees, unending
And stood to face life's upsets once again.

But now, like water, I must seek my own level
Just on my knees brings no comfort, no relief from pain.
I have been brought down to a molten mass of fiber
And lie here on my very lowest plane.

The death of my loved one leaves only desolation,
I am destroyed by ultimate pain, the very last,
My face, my body, my fingers grip
the floor for consolation
I cannot face the future, cling desperately to the past.

I see no need to try to stand without you, beloved,
I should certainly break, for I can bend no more.
If I stand again, God will have to lift me
And hold me upright by His Love and Power!

I wrote this in 1982 as I watched a good friend grieve when her husband died. I could only imagine what she was going through.

In 2004 I found myself in this same desolation. I knew this poem was right on for what life is like after my beloved spouse, my husband Bob, died. I didn't have to change one word to include it here.

In time God did lift me and held me upright to resume a life that, although empty of my loved one, continues until today as I finish this book.

I have included a poem that is a source of comfort when a loved one dies.

## A PARABLE OF IMMORTALITY

*Henry Van Dyke*

"I am standing upon the seashore, a ship at my side spreads her white sails to the morning breeze and starts for the blue ocean. She is an object of beauty and strength, and I stand and watch until at last she hangs like a speck of white cloud just where the sea and sky come down to mingle with each other. Then someone at my side, "There she goes!"

"Gone where. Gone from my sight....that is all. She is just as large in mast and hull and spar as she was when she left my side and just as able to bear her load of living freight to the place of destination. Her diminished size is in me, not in her. And just at the moment when someone at my side says, "There she goes!" there are other eyes watching her coming and other voices ready to take up the glad shout, "Here she comes"!